MICK FITZGERALD

MICK FITZGERALD

A JUMP-JOCKEY'S LIFE

MICK FITZGERALD WITH CARL EVANS

EDINBURGH AND LONDON

Copyright © Mick Fitzgerald and Carl Evans, 1999
All rights reserved
The moral right of the author has been asserted

First published in Great Britain in 1999 by
MAINSTREAM PUBLISHING COMPANY (EDINBURGH) LTD
7 Albany Street
Edinburgh EH1 3UG

ISBN 1 84018 165 6

A catalogue record for this book is available from the British Library

Typeset in 11 on 13½pt Sabon
Printed and bound in Great Britain by Butler & Tanner Ltd

Contents

Foreword

The Racing Channel and jockeys have enjoyed a close working relationship from the moment we were launched in November 1995. Since then our viewers have regularly benefited from the informed comment of top jockeys, both on the course and in the studio. In this sphere, Mick Fitzgerald has quickly established himself as a favourite with our viewers. In fact, when Mick eventually decides to retire, there is a definite opportunity for him in the media, as he is one of the most eloquent of jockeys with his colourful commentary. His famous remark after winning the Martell Grand National on Rough Quest may not have endeared him to his wife, but it certainly expressed the kind of passionate commitment and enthusiasm that jockeys like Mick bring to our sport.

Mick, like all jockeys, leads a roller-coaster life which follows a most unpredictable plot. It is part of the huge appeal of a channel like The Racing Channel, that we are privileged to share in the highs and lows of a jockey's life and watch the plot unfold on a daily basis.

Mick's autobiography will certainly be a popular read in The Racing Channel's headquarters at Corsham Street, and I feel sure that many of our subscribers will feel the same. It is always a humbling experience to read of the hard work, gritty determination and personal sacrifice that goes into the making of a top sportsman. For the majority of us, National Hunt jockeys like Mick, more than in any other sport, do things on a daily basis that we wonder at, but would never consider emulating.

Finally, all that is left for me to say is sit back, relax and enjoy a cracking read.

George Irvine
Director of Programming
The Racing Channel

I

Winning the National

Johnny Murtagh, the Irish champion jockey, once said to me, 'Mick, if you want to do this job you've got to realise you are not a normal person.'

I have reflected on those words many times and realise it is just as well I'm not a 'normal' person, a jump-jockey's lifestyle being so demanding, so rich in elation on good days, so damning on bad. Coping with the vagaries of this job is tough and there are times when I have wanted to live an ordinary life – then a good horse comes along and I acknowledge that I am one very lucky person.

Johnny elaborated on his theory by adding, 'That means you'll not be going out with your mates, drinking five or six pints at the pub and then stopping off at the chip shop on the way home.' He didn't tell me that in return for those sacrifices I would find a marvellous camaraderie, the one shared by jump-jockeys, that I would enjoy going to work, that I would achieve cherished ambitions. Above all that, above the human emotion which comes with charting a career and enjoying its ascendancy, I would take a place in sporting history by riding a Grand National winner.

When my turn came in 1996 on Rough Quest I knew I had achieved something which money could not buy and amid a welter of emotions there was humility, triumph and relief because the Grand National is more than just a race – many would class it the most important sporting occasion in Britain, concentrating the minds of millions of people. It is a tradition which is stitched into Britain's fabric; it is unique and totally irreplaceable.

I always get caught up in this Aintree heritage bit and am

fully swept along in the build-up as the big race approaches. The first tingle makes its presence felt on the Wednesday evening before the race when the BBC broadcasts a preview. Images of the programme from 1996 remain vivid; I can still see the winner's bronze trophy, sculpted by the former jockey Philip Blacker, turning on a pedestal. So, too, a list of the runners and their prices accompanied by some suitably stirring music. It was reassuring to see the names Rough Quest and M. Fitzgerald, followed by clips showing past winners and a close-up of Valentines and the front-runners streaming over the fence. How could any discerning racing fan not be moved by that? I know I was feeling the effect, the majesty of the occasion. I also allowed myself the briefest notion that I might be about to play a role, a key role, the biggest of them all, that I might win the National.

Within a few days the aspirations had become fact, the historians were adding my name to their files and I was floating through a surreal experience. My life changed and immediately became busier. There were parties, social events and charity functions. People recognised me and would stop to talk – the National is an event which most people can chat about – and since I had won a big race, owners wanted me to ride their horses. If you've got a good product to sell people will buy and winning the National was my best bit of advertising. I got plenty of coverage via television, radio and newspapers, and I was so busy in handling the media immediately after the big race that I did not get to see a very special person until late that afternoon: my father, Frank, who always travels to Aintree from home in Ireland. When I finally caught up with him the look on his face said more than a thousand words. I will never forget it. He simply put his thumbs up and said, 'You did it,' and it was as if the years of struggle had all been leading to this point, and it felt so appropriate that he was there with me.

My fiancée Jane, who I married later that year, had stayed at our home in Oxfordshire and was there in the company of many friends to greet me and my father when we got back late that evening. A banner with the words: 'Well done, Mick, what a Quest', had been hung on the side of the house, and we were soon immersed in the first of many celebratory events. We had pre-booked tickets for the 'Lesters', the Jockeys Association of

Great Britain award ceremony, which was to be held the following evening at the Hilton Hotel in London, and Jane and I received a tremendous reception when we walked in. Later, they played a re-run of the race on a giant screen which gave me a very special tingle, knowing I was sitting among the cream of my industry and winning the race which would come top of many lists.

When your luck is in, keep riding it, and at Exeter races, held 48 hours after the National, I rode two more winners before being flown to London to take part in *A Question of Sport*, a national institution in its own right and a programme which I had watched many times over the years. Being a bit of a sports enthusiast I always relished the challenge of saying the answers before the panel and now it was my turn in front of the cameras. Fortunately, the occasion did not ruffle my memory and I was 100 per cent right on the racing questions and correctly answered a few others.

My share of the prize-money from the National came to about £10,000 and it bought Jane and me a memorable honeymoon in the United States. Spin-offs included a year-long sponsorship deal with a clothing company, which paid me £5,000 and supplied a car, and I also gained a set of Top-Flite golf clubs, an odd perk for a Grand National-winning jockey, but I had become a 'celebrity' who could play a part in charity tournaments. That was no hardship since I love the game.

Yet it was my reaction to Des Lynam's question, as we stood in the winner's enclosure, which seemed to reverberate around my life, and still does. He asked: 'How does it feel to have won the National?' Without thinking but wanting to say more than just 'great', I said, 'After that, Des, even sex is an anti-climax.'

Meeting people has not been the same since. 'Oh, you're the bloke who said . . .' was all I heard for the next 12 months, and it still haunts me. When the BBC did its annual review of the sporting year it was bound to be mentioned – and it was. I regret it now for my wife's sake, because although she knows it was a throwaway line you can still imagine people thinking, 'Well, is it?' In that respect it reflects on both of us, which was never the intention.

Yet I have to admit it was exactly how I felt in those heady, memorable, euphoric moments as Rough Quest was led through the cheering crowd to Aintree's winner's enclosure. I was on such a high that nothing could have knocked me off it, and while I now reflect that I got carried away when speaking to Des Lynam, it really did feel for a few breaths as though I'd attained the peak of my life and that it would never be matched.

Comparing the feeling to sex may not have been the traditional answer, and even in these enlightened days was probably offensive to some viewers, but most adults would have gained an understanding of how it felt to have won the big race. They could identify with what I said, and it seemed I'd set a precedent because other sportsmen were asked by commentators whether scoring a goal in the cup final or winning a gold medal was as good as sex.

One thing the public hates, and increasingly so, is the old clichés: 'I was focused,' or 'Everything went according to plan.' These phrases tell the public nothing, and if you've agreed to give an interview to television or radio then you should be prepared to reveal your inner feelings. Sometimes it is difficult to find new words, especially when your head is spinning with the delight of an important victory, but the best answer is always the honest one and I gave that in reply to the question.

The danger is that you could offend someone, which I would never do intentionally, but after a big occasion like the National the adrenaline is flowing and things are said which can never be erased. For jump-jockeys the mere mention of the name Aintree is enough to create tension.

I've seen jockeys who have simply completed the course in the National, finishing miles behind the winner, who return to the weighing-room showing more joy than if they had ridden a treble or picked up a really decent prize at other meetings. And I remember clearly how affected I was when I went back to Aintree to ride Rough Quest in the 1998 National. After the jockeys are legged-up into the saddle the horses continue around the paddock a couple of times before being ushered out through the crowds towards the racecourse. I was tingling with excitement and just had to lean down to speak to the two lads leading the horse. 'You won't forget this,' I said. 'It simply doesn't come any better in this sport.'

In this book I will attempt to give an insight into a jump-jockey's life but I make no apology for looking back to find the sources for what I have achieved, partly because of their didactic value, partly to explain the twists which seem to shape sport and turn losers into winners.

My association with Rough Quest began at Nottingham in February 1995 when we finished third in a handicap chase. An inauspicious start on the face of it but the horse had been off for almost two years and was having only his second run for trainer Terry Casey after being transferred from Tim Etherington's yard.

'This horse is an absolute machine,' I said to Terry as I dismounted. 'He got tired towards the end of the race, but I believe he's got lots more to give and I would love to ride him next time.'

We duly went to Wincanton for a handicap chase over two miles and five furlongs, a trip shorter than ideal for a horse with lots of stamina, but with a week to the Festival it was ideal as a preparation for that meeting.

Terry had been learning about the horse, and we knew from his races while in his previous yard that he liked being held up in behind other horses. I talk elsewhere in this book about some horses being born leaders, but Rough Quest is very much one who prefers a back seat, ironic when you consider he was later to be thrust so firmly into the spotlight at Aintree.

'Hold him up,' said Terry, 'he'll stop if you get in front too soon.' As luck would have it we turned for home in an ideal position with a horse called Menebuck seemingly happy to give us a good tow over the final three fences. I felt before the race we were an absolute certainty to win and nothing up to that point had changed my mind, but as we came to the last, still full of running and ideally placed about two lengths behind the leader, Menebuck made a diabolical mistake and almost slowed to a walk, while my fellow put in a fine leap and landed in front.

Rough Quest immediately considered the job done and stopped trying and, despite my best endeavour, there was no response when Menebuck, his composure regained, rallied on the run-in. Obviously, this brought Rough Quest's attitude into question but I contented myself in the knowledge that had

Menebuck not suddenly handed us the lead when we didn't want it, we would have got up for a cheeky win and be feeling very happy with events.

At Cheltenham we started 16-1 for the Ritz Club Handicap Chase and I don't think I have ever seen a horse finish with so much in hand at the end of three miles and a furlong at the big meeting – let alone ridden one. He loved the soft ground that day and because the field went at a very strong gallop through-out and he had plenty of speed and stamina, the race was run to suit him. Having only 10st 3lb on his back was obviously in his favour too and he won comfortably.

The time was very respectable and I have often thought he would have gone very close had he run in the Gold Cup, which was won two days later by Master Oats. Of course no one considered him up to that standard until the Ritz victory because he had previously been beaten in ordinary handicap chases. Looking back that was no surprise – he was one of those horses who performed best in high-class races where the faster pace requires a blend of speed and stamina, which he had in abundance. As for the 'habit' of pulling himself up when he hit the front, Terry felt this was due to physical rather than mental problems, and that he sometimes felt a bit of muscle pain at the end of his races. He hung left even when winning, as he did in the Grand National, which suggests he was feeling a little discomfort somewhere, not enough to stop him galloping and jumping but the sort of minor ailment which afflicts a lot of athletes. In humans that might mean taking pain-killers, and while a drug called Bute, which has the same effect, is used in US racing it is an illegal substance in most other countries, including Britain.

Horses come in many shapes and sizes; Rough Quest is in the 'huge' category. Some horses of his dimensions can be most awkward to ride, part-elephant, part-camel, but on him it is like sitting in your favourite armchair and it is very comfortable.

With this size and comfort factor you feel as though you are sitting right into him, with plenty of head and neck in front and big quarters behind. Rough Quest is deep girthed and a very smooth walker while other tall horses leave you feeling as though you are perched above them and each step feels harsh and jarring.

His finest quality from a jockey's point of view is his jumping, which has so much scope and power. He feels as if he could tackle anything you put in front of him, no matter how big or wide, and he is clever when he gets too close to a fence, using footwork and arching his back when lesser jumpers would simply blunder through the obstacle. With these qualities I felt very confident about victory at Aintree, although the fences tempered any ideas about simply turning up and going home with the prize. If you don't treat Aintree's fences with respect you are a fool, and while they are not as big and difficult as they once were, they will still catch out those who don't do their homework; those who do can relish the challenge.

In 1996, with just 10st 7lb to carry and on ground with a nice bit of cut in it, I was as confident as I could be – it felt like it was going to be my year and even though the panel on Channel 4's *Morning Line* programme, broadcast on the day of the race, suggested he had no chance, I was not dismayed. John Francome, as I recall, said there was no way Rough Quest could win – it seems jockeys remain bad tipsters even after they retire.

My strategy had to be simple, I decided, and rather than making grand plans about how to ride the race I made life easy for myself by believing that if he stood up he would win. Getting over the tricky third fence, an open ditch, was bound to be a test but after we jumped the first fence I said to myself, 'We've no real problems here.' So it proved throughout the race, and while he got a bit close to the jump before Becher's Brook, which seemed to wake him up, the biggest danger was that he might become careless – he really did find the whole experience that easy – and by the time we came to the last we were ideally placed behind a horse called Encore Un Peu, ridden by David Bridgwater. The five lengths I had still to make up I judged to be about right on Aintree's long run-in and while 'Bridgy' kicked for home I knew I had the move covered. Closing him down as we ran towards the Elbow, the point where the running-rail bends to funnel the runners towards the winning-post, I attempted to go past on his left, knowing that if my horse began hanging in the final 100 yards he would do so in that direction. Bridgy not only covered that move, he also managed to push me wide as I switched to come around to his right; the outside. I was now out towards the middle of the course, not ideal, but I was committed by that time and knew there was no point in waiting any longer.

Rough Quest quickened under me and we went the best part of a length ahead, but then came the drift left. At first I tried to keep him straight but feeling we were clear and not wanting to pull a tired horse around, I let him go across until the running-rail put him back on a straight course and we went past the line in front.

The following moments became a fusion of heady, surging emotion, of cheering people and back-slapping colleagues. Richard Dunwoody, who had won the race twice before and knew how I would be feeling, had finished third and was now the first with congratulations. Other well-wishers began to form a swell around me and at the centre of this scrum came Geoff, Rough Quest's lad, no shatterer of joy but he had seen the finish head-on and knew his horse had drifted off a straight line. 'You won't lose it, will you?' he asked anxiously. Terry was also quickly on the scene, looking worried, but there was nothing unusual in that and in his case it was disbelief as much as fear about whether the prize was in jeopardy.

I didn't think for one minute there was any danger that the stewards might deem that I had taken Encore Un Peu's ground, a violation of the rules which could have ended in demotion to second place, but an inquiry was announced as we were being led towards the winner's enclosure. I still felt very confident as I walked into the stewards' room, but after watching a video replay my stomach began turning over and severe doubts grabbed me – it was with some relief that I heard them say the result would stand.

Later, while discussing this incident with Rough Quest's owner, Andrew Wates, he suggested it might have been better if I had pulled my whip through to my left hand and used it to keep the horse straight, either by giving him a slap down the shoulder or by waving it alongside. I maintained then that it was better to keep both hands on the reins where I had the most control; even the quickest manoeuvre of the whip would have involved putting both reins briefly into one hand, and at that point Rough Quest would almost certainly have gone hard left. While the reins are in two hands you can tug on the opposite side of the bit to the one the horse wants to travel in, while they are in one hand you are powerless to prevent a horse turning in a circle, particularly if a simple snaffle bit is being used.

I would love to win the Grand National again. Richard Dunwoody has been quoted as saying his second victory, on Minnehoma, was more satisfying than the first on West Tip. In his case the initial win came when he was just 22 and while he knew the size of his achievement he could not fully embrace it. Another eight years and seven failures went by before he was the winner again, a point at which he was able to say, 'I now know what I achieved the first time.'

In my case I am sure there are parts of my triumph which I missed. Most of us have seen a film twice and found the second viewing contains snippets we had not noticed, and that remains a probable scenario of any major event in our lives.

II
Bidding for the Top

There must be millions of youngsters who at some time dream of making a living from sport, and I was no different, although my school head teacher felt I should concentrate on getting 'a proper job'.

Watching racing on the television had stimulated my imagination and riding winners was all I wanted to do. I felt I could outride the best jockeys in the business and could not wait for the chance to prove it. Making money was not a big factor – had it been the inspiration I would not have chosen to be a jump-jockey, and since I am now passionate about golf perhaps I should have spent more time on the fairways when at school and less in the saddle. When I consider the sums earned by Mark O'Meara, the American golfer who had such a successful year in 1998, and Tony McCoy, the champion jockey, I am tempted to think racing was a mistake. O'Meara is by far the richer and, short of being struck by lightning on the fairway, runs few risks when he picks up the tools of his trade. McCoy is courting injury or worse every time the tapes go up and yet earned nothing like O'Meara last year. Yet the thrill and pleasure of riding at the Cheltenham Festival takes some beating and a Gold Cup/Champion Hurdle double might still be better than the US Masters and British Open in the same season.

As someone who prides himself on being among the top five jockeys riding at present, I am earning a good living, but I am not wealthy – and I would like to be. I come from a background where there was not a lot of money and it means I value what I have got and don't want to lose it. I am very privileged to do a job I enjoy which pays well, and I certainly aim to be solvent on the day I retire as a jockey.

In a book which looks at a jockey's life I hope I am allowed to guard my income as a private matter, but since it is public knowledge that I rode in 585 races in the 1997–98 season and was paid £86.20 a ride, it will not take long to work out I earned a little more than £50,000 in riding fees. Out of that is taken ten per cent for my agent, Dave Roberts, and I pay £8 a ride to my valet who cleans all my kit – which deducts £9,700. There are also fees for Weatherbys, accountants to the Jockey Club, who in 1998 charged 40p for every transaction on my account, and to the Jockeys Association of Great Britain which takes £1.45p per ride. That pays for membership plus insurance against accident, injury or illness and covers legal fees when we need to be represented at appeals or hearings at the Jockey Club or in a magistrates court to answer motoring offences. Away from the racecourse, jockeys are invariably clocking up the mileage on Britain's roads and our driving licences are vital. Our JA membership pays for a solicitor if we ever appear before a magistrate on a motoring charge.

On the credit side I am paid a retainer by the trainer Nicky Henderson and I receive ten per cent of prize-money when riding a winner (flat jockeys receive 7.5 per cent), and five per cent of place money, the sum given to the owners of horses which finish second or third. Once again, a jockey gives his agent ten per cent. Another bonus will hopefully come through at about the time this book is published when sponsorship of jockeys in races will become a reality. The Jockeys Association is hoping to attract one sponsor whose name will be on the breeches of every rider – it is hoped such a deal will realise about £1.5 million which will help financially and also raise jockeys' credibility.

A major expenditure comes in running a car. Costs such as petrol, servicing, depreciation (which is high because of the mileage we do) and insurance (also high because we are jockeys and have the potential to earn good money) soon become telephone numbers. If you tell an insurance company you are a jockey the quotes rocket up – it is said we have the potential to earn good money so the loss-of-earnings claim would be high, which is reflected in the premiums we pay. Talking of telephones, I run up huge bills on both my mobile and home phone and while I am not going to be seen with a begging bowl outside Cheltenham racecourse, this is not a career for people hoping to become millionaires. A good season with several big-race winners at the major festivals can bump up a jockey's earnings considerably, but a figure of around £70,000 a year would be the sort of income good riders should expect. Not bad pay while you can get it, but our careers are short, rarely lasting beyond our mid-thirties, and along the way it can take several years to become established. Once fully fledged there will be lean times, while injuries and suspensions are bound to mean the denial of a good winner now and again. As Michael Caulfield, secretary to the Jockeys Association puts it, the average jump-jockey earns the same in one year as a Premier League footballer earns in a week.

My heart goes out to a lot of lads in this game who don't have the potential to earn that kind of money – I empathise with them because I struggled too, although I was young at the time and always felt my chance would come. Other jockeys never quite make it, and while they go on riding in the hope of a big winner it is a tough life. They often make ends meet by riding horses at exercise for trainers, for which they receive a riding-out fee, and some take part-time careers out of racing. Martin Brennan's van-driving job gave the press a good story last year.

Looking back to the days when I was trying to become established, scraping by was a way of life. Each day involved a lot of hope and as much determination as I could muster, and if I was offered a ride in a race I took it without thinking about the cost, merely about the possibility that a lot of good could be involved. Hope and eternal optimism were as important as eating and it drove me on. I faltered on occasions, but hope, bolstered and encouraged by self-belief, always has to be a part of a jump-jockey's character and I will be forever grateful to Declan Murphy, the former jockey, for imparting some very sage words of advice as I clambered through the maze. 'Believe in yourself and it will pass through,' he said. He was referring to the need to instil confidence in a horse but it could also apply to humans, and while it would be a mistake to be cocky, being positive about your ability is important. Declan's career was flying at the time but he always helped me out when asked and it was a sad day when he retired while still in his prime, after suffering severe head injuries in a hurdle-race fall.

Ultimately, what all young jockeys are searching for is a good horse. They believe it will put them in the spotlight and open the door to success, although one good horse is probably not enough. You need to be associated with two or three, so the impact of your ability in the saddle has a greater chance of being noticed and even then there is little security for the youngster, who may find that having enjoyed a good ride on a horse they are then replaced by a senior jockey when the horse next runs, a process known as being 'jocked off'. When this happened to me I always tried to balance the reasons and accept the decision, especially if I felt I had made a mistake. It was harder not to feel aggrieved if I had done nothing wrong or improved the horse.

This is not to say trainers show no loyalty – far from it, and many keep an experienced horse in the yard solely for the purpose of 'giving the kids a few rides'. But occasions do arise when a youngster gets offered a ride because a senior jockey has refused it on the grounds that the horse has little chance of winning or is known to be difficult or a poor jumper. Subsequently, and perhaps because the young jockey is prepared to put in some time with the horse at home, schooling it over jumps or getting it to settle so that it conserves energy in races, the partnership may begin to show unseen ability. It is one of the harshest moments in a struggling jockey's life when they hear that the horse they had cajoled into winning or running well is to be ridden by a big-name rider, especially if the horse's next run is to be at a grade-one track. Courses such as Cheltenham and Newbury are grade one – they invariably offer better prize-money, attract better horses and receive more publicity.

The subject of being jocked off, and there have been some high-profile cases involving senior jockeys and not just youngsters, will always be contentious, but few people will deny that a top rider can be the difference between a narrow win and a defeat, and owners cannot be slated for wanting winners; it is one reason they enter the sport.

These issues, the pain and elation of the job, were unknown to me as a boy whose only link with racing came while sitting at home in Wexford watching it on the television. My interest had been fired by ponies, but since I had not sat on a thorough-bred I had no idea of the role they were to play in my life.

I didn't start riding until I was nine and it was another three years before I became aware of racing. Lester Piggott was my hero, probably because I was small for my age and felt more in tune with jockeys who rode on the flat. Being like Piggott seemed a good idea and his status as my icon grew when he forced Shadeed to victory in the 2,000 Guineas, narrowly beating Willie Carson on Bairn. I remember the television commentator eulogising about Piggott's greatness, his unique style and the number of Classic races he had won. While my home town of Camolin seemed a long way from Newmarket, I wanted to be like that. I *really* wanted to be like that. Yet it wasn't fame which entered the equation but a competitive urge in me, the desire to win big races and perform better than the other jockeys.

Perhaps it is something to do with being Irish, but I've always taken life, good and bad, at a fairly even pace, so when I did get to ride in a race, at Gowran Park in 1985, the crowds and the pressure of performing in front of the public didn't affect me. I was anxious in case something went badly wrong, but being in front of a few thousand people was no big deal. If fame was going to become an issue in my life, if the prospect of being a well-known jockey was likely to affect my attitude, it was knocked out of me, not by a person, but by circumstances, when I arrived in England seeking to make the big time.

Many young people who decide to join the racing industry are forced to move away from home and I was no different. For a teenager who had come from a very loving family and who enjoyed good relations with his parents, brother and sister, it was surprising that I was not homesick for one moment when I left Ireland. I was determined to succeed, and that goal must have overwhelmed any doubts I had about leaving my roots.

My parents, Frank and Alice, have worked hard all their life, my father as a car mechanic and my mother in the pub trade. It was long their ambition to run a pub of their own and they eventually achieved their aim some five years ago. I would have to add that the Jockey's Rest at Kilfinane is now one of the best pubs in Ireland.

Work was never a problem for my parents who grafted hard

to make life comfortable for me, my sister Elizabeth and brother John. 'If you want something,' my father would say, 'you've got to go out and earn it. It won't just happen – you've got to make it happen.' That sense of duty obviously rubbed off on us because we have never skipped a day of work in our lives, and while it is easy to say I cannot forget my father's words, his attitude to work became ingrained into us, so that even if he had never said what he did I feel sure we would have followed his example. Nonetheless, I still maintain it is one of the best pieces of advice I have been given.

My life at home was happy – I still telephone my parents three or four times a week – and so too my days at school, which perhaps is not the norm among boys who become set on a career in sport and who want nothing more than to be on the playing-field. I found lessons easy and never skipped one willingly; in fact I probably missed no more than three days during my entire school life, and only then through illness. School was fun, a good laugh, and while I did not consider myself a brainbox I picked things up quickly. This was just as well because it enabled me to gain eight honours and one pass in my final exams despite having no time for revision; after school I had to sort out the ponies we had at home and then from 6 p.m. each evening I did a four-hour shift at a local petrol station. While there I made some attempts to revise but I was always getting side-tracked and if a friend called in then the studies were forgotten.

Enjoying school was one thing but I had no wish to stay any longer than need be and left at 15 against the wishes of my head teacher, Ronnie McCormack, who came to my home and begged my parents to send me on to higher education. 'He could be anything!' pleaded Mr McCormack. 'A doctor! A vet!' Such advice was flattering but I was set on being a jockey and my father calmly said, 'If the boy wants to do it, I've got to let him.' How many parents would have had such faith in their teenage son's judgement?

The case of Angel Monserrate, who changed his name to 'Angel Jacobs' in order to ride on the flat in Britain during 1998 reminded me of this. Monserrate had been disqualified from riding by the New York Racing Authority after accepting he had smoked marijuana on the racecourse. He was later arrested in the winners' enclosure at an American track while riding under the pseudonym Carlos Castro and disappeared from racing until reappearing in Britain as an amateur by the name of Jacobs. Whether he did this because he was desperate to ride in races or because he enjoyed deceiving the authorities was never revealed, but he stood out as a talented rider – not surprising considering he had been a professional – and won five races before being exposed and disqualified again for 'misleading the stewards' and bringing racing into disrepute. His father, quoted in the *Racing Post*, said, 'When Angel was 16 he had the chance to ride in races but his mother and I thought he would be best at school. Sometimes I go to bed and think it was all our fault, we should have let him do what he wanted to do back then.' No doubt many parents understood the dilemma.

I have no regrets now that my father and I stood firm against Mr McCormack, although I was to be no teenage prodigy and could probably have stayed on to achieve further qualifications before attempting to make my mark. Looking back does no good unless it can be used as a way of correcting mistakes and I don't dwell on whether I made the right decision or not.

The future felt fairly bright at that age, and I was confident about achieving my ambition because I knew I could ride quite well through years of competing on ponies in showjumping events. Horses and ponies are a way of life in Ireland and our home was no different. My brother, sister and I all had ponies on which we competed in local shows at weekends, and now and again took hunting. Mention of the latter pastime reminds me of the day I got ready to go on my first hunt with the Island Foxhounds. I fell off going to the meet and never did take part in the hunt, but the experience I gained from these events paid dividends when I later made my first steps as a jockey.

Riding in races would have been far more daunting if I had not competed in shows, where the pressure of trying to win events and of being in the spotlight was all part of the day out. As a boy, free of any preconceived ideas and doubts, the willingness to compete seemed so natural, while another invaluable benefit was in learning to 'see a stride', the trick of knowing when a horse is about to get airborne over a jump. Learning this art at an early age, while travelling at a relatively slow pace in a showjumping ring, was vital for the bigger challenge to come: that of riding a galloping thoroughbred over birch fences in a race.

On a fantastic pony called Ballybanogue Bracken I won several decent open competitions at important shows, often gaining the prize after a jump-off against the clock, a nerve-tingling experience despite my confidence and belief in my partner. He had been bought from the tinkers for £150 and proved cheap at the price, while another pony, which we bought as a two-year-old colt, was to have an even bigger impact, although I still feel guilty that his success came after he left our yard. A pure-bred Connemara with a feisty temperament and quite a handful to break in, he came to us at about the time I was preparing to leave school and considering becoming an apprentice in a racing stable. With those commitments in mind, my father had to sell what we had at home and it was a sad day when this particular pony, who we had still not named, was taken away. I clearly remember saying to my father, 'That was the best we've had, he will be top class.' Those words came true when he later became one of Ireland's top ponies. At the age of 11 he was sold for IR£25,000 and I still feel that if I had not been so keen to become a jockey we might have uncovered his potential.

My way into racing came about through these ponies – to help pay towards their upkeep my father would take in 'breakers', ponies and horses which needed to be taught to accept a rider and which he entrusted to us to educate. Our home, about a mile out of Camolin, included some stables for these breakers and an adjacent workshop where my father plied his trade as a mechanic. It was one of his customers, while waiting for his vehicle, who noticed me working with a pony and said he knew that the trainer Richard Lister was looking for someone to help out at his stables with odd jobs at weekends and in school holidays. When this information was passed on I jumped at the chance and my father willingly got up early each morning to drive me the 13 miles to Richard's yard before returning home to eat breakfast and then heading off to do his own day's work. That evening he would repeat the journey and this went on without a single complaint from him for nearly a year. Actions like that are often taken for granted, especially when they are carried out by a parent for their teenage child, but I'll never forget the help and encouragement given by both my mother and father.

Once at the yard, and having been given my first insight into racing and the thoroughbred horse, I was bitten. From that day I have never been able to shake off the 'racing bug', a condition which seems to afflict so many people who come into contact with the way of life. The racehorse had a few more gears and a lot more speed than my father's ponies and I knew immediately that this was the career for me.

I joined Richard after leaving school in the summer of 1985 and later gained my first ride in a race, on Being Bold at Gowran Park. We finished fifth of 14 in the Thomastown colts and geldings maiden race – a respectable effort, if not an announcement to the racing world of my arrival.

It was a launching pad, however, and I certainly had the build for the job, being a shrimp who fluttered the scales to a mark of 6st 10lb. My weight did slowly creep up but I was a late developer and one year later, aged 16, I was still riding at 7st 6lb. With 21 rides in races but no winners behind me I joined another trainer, John Hayden, whose yard was near The Curragh, and there I totalled a further 60 rides in the ensuing 15 months. It was very good experience but by the end of the 1987 Flat season I had still to break my duck, three seconds and four thirds being my best efforts.

Any ambitions I had to ride an Epsom or Irish Derby winner evaporated that winter when my body finally decided to join the adult world and by my eighteenth birthday in the following May I had grown four inches since leaving school, was 5ft 10in tall and weighed 9st 7lb. Jump-racing, in which horses carry bigger weights, was now the only realistic option, and I decided the time was right to try my luck in Britain. Two reasons motivated this notion: primarily, greater opportunities, but also because in Ireland the bottom weight in a handicap can be as low as 9st 7lb. With my 7lb conditional (novice) rider's allowance that would have meant getting on the scales with all my tack at 9st and I clearly could not do that; in Britain the bottom weight of 10st gave me a better chance.

Having decided to head across the Irish Sea I rang John Jenkins, who trains at Royston in Hertfordshire. John was enjoying a purple patch at the time yet had no conditional jockey and he offered me a position. My father drove me to the airport, my mother feeling too emotional to join us on the journey, and it was certainly not easy to say goodbye before joining my flight, even though I had been living away from home for two years. The look in my father's eyes is still clear in my mind, although, as I mentioned earlier, I have never felt a moment's homesickness, the desire to get on with making a success of my career overriding all other emotions. I do miss Ireland, but only when I'm there, and the thought of turning back when I first got to England was anathema, a sign of defeat.

Knowing where to get started in any job is never easy, and a person's second or third job move is probably more important than their first. Trying to join the right yard is a dilemma for every aspiring jockey – should they join a big yard, where they will find themselves in competition not only with the number one and two senior jockeys but also very likely several other youngsters, or should they join a small yard? The latter option has the advantage of less competition from other riders but the drawback that if the yard is hit by a virus, or injury knocks out one or two horses, there could be precious little left to go racing. If the big yard is chosen there is a chance the youngster could pick up rides on the odd good horse and perhaps win a race or two, but they may equally find themselves overlooked. There will be disaffected conditional jockeys working in racing yards right now who are pondering their next move knowing it is crucial. They have to weigh up the pros and cons and decide which suits them best at the time while keeping a clear view of the long-term aim. If a small yard has a dozen horses but the form book suggests they are all capable of winning, then joining that yard could be a smart move. However, if the two senior jockeys in a big yard cannot make light weights there could be opportunities on horses near the foot of the handicap. Like racing itself, the whole thing is a gamble, but if you make a decision you should take pride in that and accept the outcome – far better that than to let someone else tell you what to do and always to blame them if it proves to be a wrong move.

Within a few weeks of arriving at John's stables in June 1988 I knew I was in the wrong place and would need to join a smaller yard in order to get opportunities to ride in races. John, who had worked through the ranks to become a middle-status jockey, had no inclination to give a youngster any special help up the ladder, preferring to book the best jockeys available, quite understandable if that was the wishes of his owners but not an attitude that was in my favour. I eventually had one unsuccessful ride for the yard, in a National Hunt Flat Race, or 'bumper', an event without hurdles or fences designed to give young jumping horses an experience of racing.

This ride hardly counts as a big event in my life, but one incident while at John's will stick in my mind. I had been to London visiting a friend and when the train stopped at Royston station I alighted with my suitcase and waited for a taxi. Two young men wandered up and asked for a cigarette, which I handed over, and while they puffed away they asked if I knew of any pubs or clubs in the area. I mentioned a couple of places and when they asked what I did for a living I told them and said I worked for John Jenkins. They wandered off and I soon forgot the encounter.

The following morning, just after six, John woke me and said there were a couple of guys downstairs who wanted to see me. This I took as a joke, John having a habit of waking us up early if he wanted a little extra job doing, so I pulled up the covers and said it was someone else's turn and that I was staying in bed for another half an hour. John persisted so I reluctantly slid out of bed, pulled on some jeans and a T-shirt and went downstairs, fully expecting that some prank was about to be played. Instead I was greeted by a scene from a war film. Outside in the yard were strategically positioned men in uniform, wearing berets and bullet-proof vests and with guns at the ready. 'Is your name Fitzgerald?' snapped a deep-voiced, mountain-sized soldier with stripes on his arm.

'Yes,' I squeaked, wide-eyed and dumbfounded.

'You asked two soldiers about security at Bassingbourne Barracks yesterday.' I looked blank. 'While at the train station,' he added.

'Soldiers? Security? I don't know any soldiers,' I replied weakly, desperately searching the recesses of my memory for clues as to why the British Army had staked out a racing stables and wanted to question 7lb-claiming-jockey Mick Fitzgerald. My interrogation continued but my answers satisfied them soon enough and, turning on his heel, the man-mountain deftly drew his finger across his throat and his colleagues relaxed, undoing their flak jackets, slinging their guns across their shoulders and heading out of the yard. I later learned that the local barracks had been breached and guns, grenades and ammunition stolen. It was just my luck to be an Irishman in the vicinity at the height of the troubles in Northern Ireland.

I had come close to getting my name in the newspapers, but for the wrong reasons, and while it was no use being maudlin about the lack of opportunities at John's, when Richard Tucker, based at Culmstock in Devon, advertised in the *Sporting Life* for a young jockey I got my application in the post. I knew nothing about his yard but I was prepared to travel anywhere for the right job and I moved there in November of the same year. Richard was a permit-holder, one of a number in Britain. They can only train their own horses or those belonging to their immediate family, but they have fewer restrictions placed on them by the Jockey Club. Licence holders can train for anyone not banned from racing but they must maintain at least six horses.

Within a month of joining Richard, I had achieved my first aim: to ride a winner. Since it came on my first ride over hurdles, on Lover's Secret at Ludlow on 11 December, I felt very happy with the move. This sense of satisfaction was enhanced when I gained another victory a few weeks later, and I remember thinking to myself, 'This job is easy, why the hell didn't I make the move sooner?' I had no idea of the lean times ahead and that it would take another 18 months to revisit the winner's enclosure. That barren period will always ensure I keep success in perspective. Had it gone on much longer it would have been another jockey who won the National on Rough Quest – I was planning to go to New Zealand.

Failure to add to my total of two wins in that period caused a range of emotions. There was the rebellious stage, not unusual in teenagers perhaps, where my attitude was 'I don't give a toss about this game'. Of course I did but it seemed a suitable way of countering disappointment. Going to the pub and drinking beer was fun, it was easy and I didn't have to impress anyone while I was doing it. Getting in late for work was wrong, and I knew it, but surely it didn't matter if I wasn't getting rides in races, if I was being left behind in the contest to make a name, to become a jockey.

In the summer of 1989, part way through this trough but before it had become an issue, I moved to Somerton in Somerset and joined Ron Hodges, a licensed trainer with more horses than Richard and a reputation for giving youngsters chances to ride in races. Wally Irvine, who later retired through injury, and Chris Maude, who was my age and looking to get established, were already at the yard and while they would be in competition with me for rides it seemed this was the right move. I was wrong. Wally got most of the rides, while Chris, whose mother now trains point-to-pointers in that area, had a few contacts in local stables and was making the most of those on a fairly regular basis. It seemed I was the one who couldn't get going and in the following 12 months I had just a handful of rides on horses who had no chance of winning even if they had joined in halfway through the race.

In a situation like that, and whatever the business, you have two choices. You can give up, take a back seat and quit, or you can try even harder, put in extra hours, smile more broadly and sweat more freely. For a young jockey that would entail riding out and schooling horses for other trainers during lunch breaks or days off and phoning yards in a bid to secure rides in races, even though rejections can be embarrassing and demoralising. It might take only one good schooling session to change a career, but equally you could school a thousand horses and achieve nothing.

Looking back it is easy to be critical of myself, but at that age, still a teenager in a hurry, I wanted tangible results, not mere possibilities, and as demoralisation became dangerously more imminent I began to question whether it was worth the struggle. Besides, while I wasn't afraid to ride any horse in any race, any spare rides would be on useless, perhaps dangerous nags – if they were any good a well-known jockey would be looking to ride them. For me, a young man who wanted to get to the top, there seemed no point in going through a lot of hassle for one ride on a horse which had already shown itself to be incapable.

I was good, I felt, but not a magician. It was easier to drink beer and forget my frustrations.

Clearly this attitude was wrong, but I cannot say I regret it completely since it was partly the result of being relaxed about life, of being laid-back, and that, I believe, is a quality which now stands me in good stead. Sure, I was becoming increasingly fed up at not getting rides in races, but I wasn't throwing things around or having outbursts of pent-up frustration in public. I was just losing the will to struggle against the tide.

Part of the problem was that I got on so very well with Ron and his wife Amanda, who allowed Chris Maude and me to live with them in their house. It was a very pleasant, easy-going time, ideal, you might think, for building a relationship with the boss in order to further my career. Strangely enough it worked in reverse, although it seems churlish now to criticise Ron, a man who was so friendly to me. A typical day would end all sitting round in the living-room, watching television or cracking jokes together like one big happy family. It was too cosy and when I suddenly realised that I knew it was counting against me and that I had to get away.

Why Ron did not give me more opportunities in races I still don't know. Perhaps it was because I hadn't shown I was committed enough, but as I was living with him, and he could see everything I did, what more could I do? How do young people get up the ladder? Surely living with the boss and having a laugh with him was as good a way of ingratiating myself as anyone could imagine. But it had its disadvantages too – because we knew each other so well, I felt as though I could never surprise him by doing something extra. Familiarity was creating apathy towards my goal of being a jockey; why would he want to change a routine which seemed to suit us both?

Most trainers will help their staff get a taste of riding in races but they don't want the entire payroll begging for a jockey's licence. A person who can muck out, ride, work and school horses, groom in the evenings, work weekends and travel to the races, is an essential cog in a racing yard. If they break bones riding in a race they are off work and of no use.

There must have been countless cases of youngsters being steadily discouraged from thinking about becoming a jockey in the hope that they stop wanting to be one, settle down to life as a member of staff and remain as an employee in the yard. Good staff are at a premium now as never before. Of course, a really talented young jockey who can claim a weight allowance of up to 7lb for being a novice, is worth using in races. Then there are those who want the chance, but are not rated good enough. They might get a few rides in races and get frustrated when they don't get more. Often they just don't have the aptitude. In my case I don't think Ron considered me good enough.

I have no bitterness in that respect, because an opinion of talent is subjective and I've proved him wrong. Yet he did not tell me I wasn't good enough – if he felt I wouldn't make the grade I should have been told. He didn't give me one solitary good ride while I was there. I rode no more than ten horses in the season and they were all absolute rubbish. How could anyone, let alone a teenager with no understanding of life's ups and downs, be committed about riding such bad horses. Some of them were so awful they had very little chance of completing the course.

Apathy crept in and I really didn't care too much about the job, so when one serious occasion turned into high farce I saw no point in missing out on the fun. The local hunt were to meet at the yard and Ron asked me, Chris and Wally to act as drinks ushers, so after riding two quick lots we dusted ourselves off and assembled in the kitchen to be supplied with trays of port and brandy. It was a fine morning, near Christmas, and a really festive sight as the scarlet-coated huntsman and masters and members of the hunt gathered in the yard. Hounds sat in the sun or nosed around, horses pawed the ground, terriers strained at leashes and foot-followers chatted, supped port or brandy and ate mince pies.

Dutifully the three young jockeys spread out, mingled through the crowds handing out drinks and met at an agreed point, conveniently out of sight of the congregation. Chris had a couple of glasses still full on his tray and Wally and I had too, so we decided that if the hunt could have a drink on this bright, cold day, so could we. I am pretty sure we had not eaten much that morning and the delicious liquid hit the bottom of my stomach as soon as I emptied the first glass. Back to the kitchen we went, filled the trays with fresh supplies and set off again, having agreed to meet at the same point. Again, we had surplus drinks on our trays and warmed by the first intake, we furtively sloshed back a second. This exercise was repeated at least once more, so that by the time the huntsman's horn blew we were feeling distinctly mellow – in fact we were half-pissed.

Clearing the empty glasses scattered around the yard was like a scene from a pantomime and although there was a third lot of horses to be ridden our stomachs were rumbling. With Ron having gone off for the day we decided to drive to the pub for lunch. I got behind the wheel of my new car, a battered Datsun recently bought from Chris, and we spun out of the yard and across the fields, a well-used back route to the local boozer. Piling through the door just before midday, we sunk several more glasses of brandy each, managing to break three or four in the process, and finally staggered out, bleary-eyed, into fading sunlight at closing time. The third lot of horses had been long forgotten.

Spinning the wheels into action we headed back in the general direction of home. I was revved up, Chris bleated incessantly about the speed we were going, Wally was silent in the back, and when our serpentine journey, punctuated by several handbrake turns, resulted in the car getting wedged against a hedge, he disappeared out of the car, unbeknown to his two companions. To this day Chris and I do not remember his exit but having got the car rolling forward again we got back to the yard, looked at each other and said in unison: 'Where's Wally?' Why that should be so funny I have no idea – I just remember lying on the lawn in the main yard, doubled up with laughter, begging Chris to shut up because I couldn't breathe, while he rolled around too, helplessly convulsed.

The admonishment of Jane, Ron's head girl, brought an air of reality to the caper but I was in no state to absorb what she was saying. I just knew I felt bloody uncomfortable when waking up in the tack-room some seven hours later, shoeless and my hair thick with hoof oil and marmalade, a recrimination by my colleagues who had to ride out and groom my horses at evening stables. Further penance for the three naughty boys included getting up two hours earlier the next day to muck out every horse in the yard before the other staff came in. My head hurt and I felt sick lifting sackfuls of droppings and urine-drenched bedding – but I still smile today when I think of that escapade.

I would not recommend any aspiring jockey trying to emulate this behaviour but I was losing hope and did not care about the consequences. Ron was Ron about the incident, he took it in good spirit, which was typical of the man. I regard him as a friend and while it cannot be said he helped me become a jockey, it was while being employed by him that I met Ray Callow, who trained under permit nearby and used Ron's gallops. Ray, or rather his horses Sunset Sam and Duncan Idaho, were to be the catalysts which turned my career around, and while Ron wouldn't want any credit, it was a lesson in life.

Just prior to this dramatic change in fortune I came close to quitting British racing. Through John Nicholson, the brother of event rider Andrew, I made enquiries about going to New Zealand. If nothing else I could see a bit of the world and take my trade with me. Andrew said there were good opportunities for young jockeys and I thought it was a challenge which would suit me.

Life changes in the space of a few words and mine did when Ray asked if I would like to ride a horse of his in a selling hurdle at Hereford. 'Selling' races are usually contested by very moderate horses and the winner is offered for sale at an auction in the winners' enclosure. They are designed to give mediocre horses a winning opportunity – good ones don't take part for fear they will be snapped up at the subsequent sale. It was May Bank Holiday in 1989, Sunset Sam was the horse, the result was a win and for good measure I beat Graham Bradley on a horse of Martin Pipe's. New Zealand was suddenly less important and that win gave me the boost to get a grip on myself and focus on what I was good at and how I might utilise my strengths. I had rediscovered the adrenaline which I'd felt when watching Piggott ride Shadeed. It was a kick up the backside and a rekindling of the buzz which makes race-riding such an addiction. It was enough to send me on my way, and that meant sorting myself out and changing jobs to break the chain of cosy routine which had become the norm at Ron's.

Buoyed by the Sunset Sam victory I again had a clear goal and knew it was only going to be achieved by leaving Somerton.

Gerald Ham, another Somerset trainer based in Axbridge, had just enjoyed two very good seasons and had a vacancy which seemed to suit a young jockey who was desperate for a positive move. Now aged 20, and with the princely total of three winners to my name, I had no time to waste. Teenagers who ride winners tend to get a bit of publicity simply because of their youth, but once a rider leaves their teens behind questions are asked as to why they are taking so long to get established. Such issues are less important if a rider is associated with a successful yard and quietly getting rides, but I knew I had not even reached base camp, let alone started scaling the heights.

With Gerald, a gentleman through and through, I began to make ground, and having ridden a few winners for the stable my confidence began to grow. Phoning other stables in a bid to supplement my rides began to reap some rewards and it was to be a real break when I noticed in the paper that a horse due to run at Sandown the following day, called Rafiki and trained by Jackie Retter, had no jockey alongside its name. Getting a ride at one of Britain's premier courses, which I had yet to do during some two and a half years in the country, would have been almost as good as partnering a winner, so I had plenty of incentive to make my bid to get on the horse.

In West Country racing, Jackie was becoming known as a skilful trainer who could get results from horses which had been failures in other stables, but few can have realised then that she would enjoy one of the steepest success rises in racing during the 1990s. I certainly knew who she was, but the recognition was not mutual when I spotted her at Newton Abbot races later that day and brazenly walked up and introduced myself, asking for the ride on Rafiki at the same time. She seemed taken aback, and while I would have rung that evening had I not seen her it might have been easier to dismiss my request on the phone. Instead she said she would think about it, and subsequently contacted Gerald to check out my credentials. He put in a good word for me and I was chuffed to get the booking.

Things went from good to fantastic when I asked Rafiki to quicken going up Sandown's finishing straight and he responded to win by five lengths, an incredible feeling even though it was the last race of the day and most people were heading for the carparks by the time we entered the winner's enclosure. This victory encouraged Jackie to give me further chances and I ended the season riding four winners for her while still based with Gerald. In addition, Rafiki was by far the best horse I had ridden up to that point and the prospect of getting on him again filled me with optimism and confidence, which, as I say more than once in this book, are absolutely crucial qualities in a jockey.

By the beginning of the following season Jackie had made me a very generous, and in some ways remarkable, offer: to become first jockey at her stable. With every stable at her yard full, a total of some 20 horses, and plenty more waiting to come in when a vacancy arose, it was a prized job offering quality and a fair bit of quantity too. Far more experienced jockeys than me would have been delighted with the offer, yet here was I, a 7lb claimer with about a dozen winners, being invited to take the position. It was a great chance and while I did not regard myself as the complete jockey I knew that if I worked hard we would get results.

Without doubt Jackie remains one of the best trainers I have been employed by, but while praising her to the hilt, I know we complemented each other. There was a chemistry between us when it came to looking after and extracting the best from racehorses, and since we were both relatively young for our jobs there was stacks of enthusiasm being generated. To use a metaphor, she could turn horses inside out, discovering what made them tick or what ailed them. It was a natural talent and one which she revelled in while working with a stable of that size. If she had been given 100 horses Jackie could not have given each one the individual care which was her forte. While some trainers handle those quantities very successfully by delegating while retaining overall control, that would not have worked for Jackie, one of her weaknesses being that she loved her horses so much she had to adopt a hands-on role even though other aspects of the job needed her attention.

Without really planning how I could fit into this regime, we formed a working partnership in which Jackie did her thing and I did mine. The results are reflected by the successes we enjoyed on the racecourse in the seasons 1991–92 and 1992–93. Jackie's strength lay in uncovering the secrets of equus while mine lay in galloping, schooling and doing the preparatory work before a horse ran, and since I was now working with these horses every day we had a useful advantage when I rode them in races. We worked independently but would combine ideas when it came to studying form, watching races and making entries, and one of our strengths was in working with difficult or shy horses.

The halcyon days I enjoyed with Jackie were ultimately the route to the top jockeys' table, and when Nicky Henderson invited me to join his stable I was torn emotionally but knew I had to grab the chance with both hands. My career had passed through base camp and on to the upper reaches of the mountain where I would soon be touching pinnacles. I have not reached them all yet but it was Jackie's faith which helped me to the point I am now.

It saddens me still that her career went in the opposite direction and she eventually handed in her licence. I know she was hurt when I left, feeling that I was breaking up a winning team, but that sort of disappointment happens regularly in business and has to be put to one side. She forgave me and I subsequently rode winners for her, as I have done for every trainer for whom I have worked, bar Richard Tucker. Perhaps Jackie reached a point at which she had shown she could compete with the best yards in Britain and had lost the drive which is needed to slog away seven days a week. Ultimately she decided to pack in training, a sad loss of talent.

Decisions, decisions. Jackie made hers and young jockeys are faced with a multitude too. It is not a job which involves turning up for work and merely getting on with the daily workload – every horse and each race involves numerous possibilities so it is hardly surprising mistakes are made. Yet perhaps the most important choice is knowing where to make a start as a jockey and when to move on. It involves decisions which can affect a youngster's career.

III

The Horses

It could be assumed that horses simply become tools of a jockey's trade, but I have never taken that view. No matter how frustrating they are, no matter how often they hurt me, I still love them.

You can never take a horse for granted and it would certainly be pretty dull if we could. Each has its own characteristics and when we meet them we can never be sure how they will react. They have good and bad days and while they possess many human qualities they have shunned most of our failings. They work for us, willingly generally, and yet they have the strength to resist. Few animals match their grace and power.

Anyone who rides or owns horses will have their favourites and in that respect I'm no different. I really, really, look forward to riding some horses. Getting up in the morning when I'm due to ride one of my favourites is always easier. There's a sense of anticipation, a feeling that the day will be a good one – we might not win, but the special horse is always a pleasure to ride. Building a rapport with them takes time and is therefore more rewarding once it is achieved. In jump-racing this can often mean an association over many seasons – on the flat a good horse has a future at stud and may race only a handful of times.

The first horse I became attached to after receiving my jockey's licence was Sunset Sam, trained by Ray Callow, and a key factor in the success I enjoy today. That was enough to endear me to him, but he was also a character. A bay horse, 16 hands high but nothing special to look at, his form was not great but he was definitely his own man, a characteristic which most of us respect in humans, even if it can prove inflexible on occasions. In a race it would mean allowing him to travel at his own pace and generally near the rear of the field for the early part of the contest. He jumped well enough, so there was not much wrong with him physically, but he did require time to warm up and taking it easy early in a race was his way of doing so. He couldn't tell us his joints ached or his back was troublesome, the sort of everyday complaints which afflict most athletes, but he knew what suited him and we knew it was no use trying to dictate something different. When we tried to ride him closer to the pace, within a horse or two of the leader, he was just that little bit less willing and unable to produce more power when other horses quickened in the final half mile.

However, if he was happy he was a joy to ride. Over the last few hurdles he seemed to sense the race was coming to a conclusion and while he was slow against good horses, in his class he could really go past his rivals.

His stablemate, Duncan Idaho, won five times for me the following season, including my first televised success in a race at Uttoxeter on Midlands National day. Channel 4 cameras were broadcasting as M. Fitzgerald, claiming 7lb, galloped to victory with Richard Dunwoody and Peter Scudamore coming in behind on the placed horses – that added lustre to the occasion.

Like Sunset Sam, Duncan Idaho had his idiosyncrasies. He too had to be held up in the pack during his races and needed muddy ground before producing his best. Assessing the underfoot requirements of different horses is a key part of a trainer's job, but knowing why some like mud and others prefer firm ground is still largely unexplained; breeding and confirmation, a horse's shape and structure, are often key elements, but in Duncan Idaho's case it was largely because he had terrible forelegs, ones which were always showing signs of heat and puffiness. Soft, muddy turf, free of jar, helped him extend when galloping.

Initially he wasn't the greatest jumper and he was hardly an ideal shape, but Ray did a fine job in picking races when the horse was well and he consequently soared up the handicap collecting victories on the way.

Training and racing horses is a fascinating business because of the many challenges, and apart from assessing a horse's ground preferences there are other imponderables which can mean the difference between winning and losing. Some horses prefer galloping left-handed, others to the right, some perform best in blinkers, others in a visor, some respond to very gentle handling, others seem clueless without assistance from the saddle.

Duncan Idaho, as I have mentioned, needed soft ground and to be allowed to travel at the back of the field in the early part of a race. In his case the reluctance to be near the front too soon was almost certainly down to his physical problems – lobbing along, slipstreaming other horses, gave him time to warm up. I suppose we could have gone for a thrash round the track before his races, filling his muscles with blood and his lungs with oxygen, but that would also have wasted valuable reserves of energy, so I simply had to ride him patiently and hope that while we were conceding ground there would be plenty in the tank when the race began in earnest. Since he was a three-miler, there was generally time to execute this style of racing to our advantage.

Other horses simply must be at the head of affairs: Desert Orchid has been the most famous recent exponent of this style of racing and in his case I believe he was naturally a leader. Horses like him don't perform so well when jammed into a bunch where their innate exuberance is dulled.

I rode against Dessie on just one occasion, at Wincanton when I was partnering Smarties Express for Ron Hodges – he was a good, tough horse and I later rode him to finish second in the Mildmay of Flete Chase, my first serious attempt to pick up a prize at the Cheltenham Festival.

With Dessie in attendance a big crowd had turned up and defeat seemed out of the question for the star act – the rest of us could put up a good show and race for second prize-money, but realistically Dessie would have to take the wrong course if we were to win.

Should jockeys try spoiling tactics in a bid to unsettle a horse as good as Dessie? Finding an opponent's Achilles heel can bring rewards and there is nothing wrong if the tactics don't break racing's rules. For instance, if a fancied horse needs a test of stamina there is nothing wrong in a rival setting a slow pace in a bid to catch their opponent flat-footed in a sprint finish.

Attempting to dethrone Dessie in that particular race was a

wholly different situation. We knew he would jump off quickly and set a strong gallop and, short of tying his legs together, there was no way we could prevent that. There were not many runners, so we could hardly box him in, and even if there had been 20 of us it would have been easier for kids to hang on to an eel while playing in the sea. He always got a good start because he was so keen to race and had we tried to box him in before the tapes went up the starter would have refused to let us go until each runner had a fair chance of a clean break.

Dessie had many attributes but a key one was his ability over a variety of distances. Good three-mile chasers could not sap his stamina, good two-mile chasers could not go quickly enough to burn him off. Those who tried were up against a brilliant jumper who saved energy by his fluency at the fences – consequently most burnt up their own reserves of energy when trying to upset his front-running style and it was they who ended up losers.

A similar situation continues today in many races involving Martin Pipe's horses; because he believes in getting them very fit for their races, and because he likes to see them making the running, they are generally towing the field along. Few have Dessie's outstanding qualities, and it is possible to unsettle them by taking them on, but while this might mean the Pipe runner is defeated it can mean defeat too for the horse which has taken up the challenge. As jockeys we are all quite happy if another horse, a headstrong one perhaps, takes on the Pipe horse, encouraging it to expend an unnecessary amount of energy and thereby leaving it vulnerable to a challenge in the closing stages.

Broughton Manor, a mare trained by Jackie Retter and who provided me with seven victories over fences, is another name which instantly comes to mind when I think about those all-important days when I was still a conditional jockey trying to establish myself. Winning on her at Kempton, one of Britain's premier tracks, was an ideal advertisement and her exemplary jumping was good for my confidence and showed people that I could ride over fences, most of my victories to that point having come over hurdles.

Training Broughton Manor was not easy since she could be temperamental – 'mareish' as we say in the trade. Yet when the tapes went up for the start of a race that temperament was put to good use and she would battle to beat other horses. It seems strange that a peaceful herbivore like the horse, an animal whose instincts are to wander the plains and who offers no threat to other creatures, should find such fighting qualities when it comes to racing. Perhaps we are simply putting human emotions into the equation when we say horses 'battle', perhaps the signs of wanting to fight are being confused with their instincts to be dominant and protective among their own kind. Stallions will fight among themselves to decide who mates with the most mares, the mares will fight with wolves and bears if it means protecting their young, senior members of a herd will scold youngsters.

Whatever the horse's thoughts in a situation which we later describe as 'giving their all', or 'battling to beat the other horse', it is certainly not a facet of all racehorses. Those who do 'battle' seem to tense under you as they power through their shoulders and quarters, grabbing the ground and pushing against it with their hooves. The position of the neck and head, thrust forward, is reminiscent of the boxer crouching before launching one more volley of punches. Conversely, those who are not trying give their reluctance away by not stretching their necks and leaning on the bit, subsequently feeling 'light' in your hands. There is no element of power under the saddle since they are not pushing hard through their hindquarters.

The alternative, the horse which tries and tries, might not win and they invariably get nothing like the credit they deserve, which is one of the sadder aspects of my life as a jockey. There are occasions when I wish I could get greater recognition for a horse who would have given his life for the cause but was simply beaten by a superior rival. You really get attached to such honest horses and want them to get the praise given to those who find winning easy. How true this seems to be of human athletes too. We regularly hear people bemoaning the coverage given to super-gifted stars like Ronaldo, Dettori and Schumacher while less-talented players, who put in just as much if not more effort, get far less media interest. Were they to get more coverage it would boost their morale and possibly their chances of a little sponsorship or a bit of elevation among their peers.

Broughton Manor, Sunset Sam, Duncan Idaho and other West Country-trained horses, helped me get going, but the first high-quality horse I rode was Henry Mann, trained by Simon Christian. Being asked by his owners, Lynn and Judy Wilson, to ride a horse of such ability was an endorsement of my rise through the ranks, a sign that people felt I could handle the pressure of big races. It was a good break.

As a hurdler Henry Mann had won the Joe Coral Hurdle final at Cheltenham and he subsequently went back to the Festival the following year and finished second to Tipping Tim in the Ritz Club Chase while still a novice. Given reasonable progress he looked capable of entering the Gold Cup picture, so I felt very proud and excited when I was asked to ride him in a handicap chase at Newbury in the autumn of the following season.

The feeling of loss and disappointment when we finished last was almost unbearable. I remember thinking, 'Oh my God, what have I done to deserve this?' To be so optimistic one moment and so utterly beaten the next was a really harsh moment for an ambitious young jockey who knew how important and how rare a good break could be.

Returning through the crowds before I climbed out of the saddle, I experienced a raft of thoughts: would I be blamed, could I have done anything different, how would the owners and trainer react? I felt sure it was not my fault, but as I am my own fiercest critic I was beginning to have my doubts.

I received no blame and simply shared the moment of despondency with the horse's owners before going back to the weighing-room, but I couldn't help but analyse every aspect of the race for the rest of that day. Getting to sleep was a relief, but the following morning my mind was racing again, as it always does when I feel the need to weigh up a disappointment. My way of analysing this, of coping with it before getting back into action, is to break the performance down into compartments: did the horse feel keen or lively going to the first fence, how did he jump, how did he handle the ground? In Henry Mann's case he showed no life from the start and while it was disappointing I was able to console myself that I had done all I could.

It transpired that the horse was good on his day but

occasionally disappointing; pinpointing that in advance was impossible, the person that could get inside a horse's mind to gain such information would be a millionaire and no trainer has perfected the art, although some are better at it than others.

Henry Mann then went to Cheltenham for the Timeform Chase, a well-known Gold Cup trial, and while I was prepared for the worst, I hoped for a good bit better than that and I was not disappointed. He ran a blinder, jumped like a stag, galloped well and finished a close-up fourth to Sibton Abbey, but post-race optimism was muted in the following weeks when his legs caused problems and he joined the list of good horses whose physical frailties were to shorten their careers.

To become a success as a jump-jockey you need good horses that can perform in top races, and not just occasionally. You need to be there on the big stage year in and year out, and that requires help from several horses. Once you are proven as a jockey who has experience of the big time your name goes into the hat when spare rides become available, perhaps because a horse's regular jockey is injured or suspended or perhaps because they are riding at another meeting.

If any one horse put me into that bracket, and bearing in mind the role others played, it has to be Raymylette, trained by Nicky Henderson. Not only was Raymylette my first Cheltenham winner, he also won good races the following season, so he provided quantity as well as quality. His importance to me can be gauged by the fact that only two horses are allowed to be portrayed in our living-room – Jane and I don't want our house to become a shrine to the horse, despite its role in our lives. Above the fireplace hangs an oil painting of Rough Quest jumping at Aintree and on an adjacent wall is Raymylette leaping the last fence before winning the Cathcart Chase. That victory will always shine in my memory, and that brilliance is super-enhanced by the misery I incurred 24 hours earlier.

When I say the name Remittance Man, lovers of horse racing will immediately think of one of the best horses of the nineties. He was a spectacular jumper and a champion who twice won at the Cheltenham Festival, recording victories in the Arkle and Queen Mother Chases. I admired the horse too, and while he was generally ridden by Richard Dunwoody – who had become associated with him before I joined the Henderson yard – it was a wonderful moment when the boss called me in and said I could ride him in the Queen Mother Chase of 1994, 'Woody' having been suspended for a fracas at Nottingham where he had effectively squeezed Adrian Maguire around the wing of a hurdle.

Remittance Man had missed the previous season through injury but the Governor had done a wonderful job getting him fit to win at Kempton on his reappearance, when he beat Deep Sensation, a top-class horse trained by Josh Gifford, giving a performance which made him favourite for the Cheltenham race. To that point I had not been given such a high-profile opportunity so it was another giant leap for me and, breathless with excitement, I clearly remember looking Nicky in the eye and saying, 'I won't let you down Governor.'

The meeting didn't start very well for the yard, a portent for future races as it transpired, with Barna Boy virtually getting knocked over at the first in the opening Supreme Novices' Hurdle. The following day everything seemed set for the big race: with Travado backing up Remittance Man, the yard had two major players in the most important two-mile chase of the year.

The bigger a horse's reputation, the bigger we seem to presume a horse's size, and no end of people have talked of Remittance Man as 'a big horse'. Far from it, he was compact but very neat and athletic and at the gallop it was like sitting at the controls of a luxury vehicle. I've not flown a Lear jet or steered an ocean racing yacht, so I'll have to limit the analogy to cars, and Remittance Man was very smooth but with the power of a high-performance sports car.

With those sort of options at my disposal, and notwithstanding the fact that his rivals were also coasting in second gear, I could not have been happier as we went past the packed stands with a circuit to run while the Queen Mother watched and waited to hand her trophy to the winner.

Running up the hill we jumped the ditch effortlessly and were soon turning the corner and heading down towards the third-last fence, where the pace usually quickens a notch or two. I was happy with my position but because, as always, at this point the horses who had been at the back began closing up and fanning around the leaders in a bid to get a good look at this tricky fence, I gave Remittance Man a little squeeze, shortening my reins, lowering myself in the saddle, asking him to give a little more effort and, for the first time, a doubt crept into the equation. He didn't respond as I had hoped, and while he was giving it a good shot, I could feel myself clutching at the pre-race optimism which was just starting to ebb. 'C'mon, c'mon, c'mon,' I was saying to myself, 'don't let this slip – find a spark, find a turn of foot, find hope.'

The fence seemed to grow, it was sucking us in and we all wanted to get it out the way, to fly it and land running towards the home turn. At this pace a mistake would mean defeat, but I was on the greatest jumper in Britain and as I saw a long stride I asked him to go and never for one second considered there would be any outcome but another superlative jump.

In the next few seconds we had entered the books as fallers and I was sliding across the turf. As I think about that moment now I still feel choked and it hurts to describe the following hours.

My first recollection, one which is so clear, is of sitting in the grass, the sound of hooves fading as the crescendo from the grandstands rose and thinking to myself, 'What on earth have I done?' Usually in those moments after a fall you curse and blame yourself or the horse, or another runner. This time there was nothing. I was in shock. It might seem stupid, horses being made of flesh and blood, but I could not believe that he hadn't got airborne, hadn't taken off when I wanted but had put in another stride which had taken him far too close to the fence with the inevitable consequence that he crashed over.

I've not experienced a lower point in my career, and the misery was not helped as I climbed into a Land Rover for a lift back and heard the commentary as the race drew to a climax. Travado, under Jamie Osborne, was still there with a chance and they were climbing the hill to the winning-post. I was screaming for all I was worth, willing him to victory, knowing it would be great for the yard but with that instinctive feeling that it would deflect some of the attention away from my fall. Gloom settled on gloom as it became apparent he had just failed to beat the exceptional Viking Flagship.

I met the Governor back at the weighing-room and tried to explain what had happened. He was passive and philosophical, while owner Tim Collins said generously, 'As long as you're okay and the horse is okay, that's all that matters.' I wasn't sure it was all that mattered and felt pretty worthless at that point.

Having reached home that evening the self-interrogation started, the grilling, the self-analysis, the need to inspect every scrap of evidence in a bid to solve an issue which could not be righted. That didn't stop me viewing a video of the race – from the top of the hill to the fall – at least 50 times; that's my way of handling it. Other jockeys might prefer to watch it once, put it out of their mind, and carry on, but I need to tortuously inch my way back over the ground until I have an answer and I usually find one, or believe I do.

On this occasion the reality was agonisingly clear and I knew I had to take the blame. As I watched the race again and again the truth could not be avoided that the horse was not going well enough and did not have the reserves of energy to be able to make such a mighty leap. That was the one crucial thing and I kept repeating to myself, 'You weren't going well enough,' until it was jammed in my brain, a lesson which I would hopefully never forget. Since then I've watched that fence with more than a passing interest. While it is the scene for a fair number of falls I believe many are caused because horses don't have the reserves to put in a big jump. This is not always obvious to the jockey because the downhill run gives the impression that the horse is still galloping on the bit and within itself.

In hindsight I should have sat still and allowed Remittance Man to fiddle the fence, which would have conceded ground but kept us in the race, far better than the humiliation of putting such an excellent jumper on the floor.

Strangely enough, I've often been in similar situations since, galloping fast into a fence near the end of a race and always two options enter my thoughts: do I go 'shit or bust' and attempt to get a really bold leap at the fence, or do I take a conservative stance and let the horse fiddle, albeit the chances are we will lose ground? In that Remittance Man ride such issues never entered my head and the whole thing remains like a bad dream to this day.

Back to Raymylette, who was about to appear cavalry-like on the horizon and pick up not only my Festival – my general mental well-being too I guess – but also that for the whole yard which had so often been a provider of Cheltenham winners in the past.

I would have to say that Raymylette was my favourite horse, even above my Grand National winner Rough Quest. A big chestnut horse, Raymylette was very keen but nervous and fractious and he needed to be trained on his own to prevent him becoming gassed up by the excitement of being with other horses. In his races he was invariably happiest out in front, galloping with real zest.

Being a free runner like that could have led to jumping difficulties – a horse which likes blasting along can often hit fences simply because he is so keen to gallop he doesn't consider jumping to be an issue and is prone to flip over – but in Raymylette's case the speed he galloped at was used to give him mighty leaps too.

He was the most perfectly balanced horse it has been my privilege to ride and I remember thinking after we had jumped two fences in the Cathcart Chase, and bearing in mind it was the first time I had ridden him in a race, 'This is a dream machine.'

No one in the yard had realised at that stage just how good a horse he was. He had run only twice over fences, at Leicester and Warwick, winning novice chases under Richard Dunwoody but not beating too many tough competitors in the process.

All was going well when we started on the downhill run to the third-last fence – the one where Remittance Man and I had hit the deck so spectacularly the previous day. It is easy to say now, but I believe those two rides taught me more about racing over fences than the previous two years had done.

We reached the fence on the same stride as I had done 24 hours earlier, in other words our take-off position was once again a fair way from the fence, but this time I just sat very still and he went 'whoosh', picking up to leap the fence when he was ready and not because I was dictating terms. He absolutely flew it.

A quick flash went through my mind and I remember thinking to myself, 'Well there you go, everything you considered while watching the video the night before has been confirmed. I did the wrong thing then, the right thing now.'

The fundamental difference was that Raymylette had the gas to make a big leap at the fence, but rather than attempt to guess that, I had let him make the decision. Previous to that telling moment I would have said you have to do something by way of a signal to the horse as a fence approaches, it might be a little squeeze in the flanks with your heels, a little click with the tongue or a shortening of the reins, perhaps a tap down the shoulder with the whip; but if a horse is going willingly forward the motto must be to sit quietly.

Yogi Breisner, the well-known event rider and one of the finest tutors when it comes to teaching jumping to humans and horses, said to me afterwards: 'When you jump a fence never be afraid to do nothing, it's generally better than pulling or tugging a horse around. Have confidence and the horse will do it.'

With that fence out the way I pushed on for home in pursuit of my first Festival winner and, after jumping the second-last fence, I could hear the wave of sound coming from the grandstands as the crowd began to shout. A fancied Irish runner, Buckboard Bounce, under Irish champion jockey Charlie Swan, was beginning to close, a sure way of doubling the decibel level, but we deflated their aspirations with a really extravagant jump at the last and while Raymylette was tired on the run-in we held on for victory.

A Cheltenham Festival winner had been my biggest ambition for so many years that after the events of the previous day I was very relieved to have finally achieved it. Nicky's face as we returned to the winner's enclosure was one of total elation. Almost three days of racing at the game's biggest event had gone by and he had been without a winner to that point, an enormous amount of pressure for a trainer who had gone there with such high hopes. As I dismounted amid the cheers and clapping from people banked up right around the enclosure, he simply said, 'You don't know what this means to me.'

No other defining moment has shaped my career as a jockey quite like that one, and Raymylette's subsequent successes cemented the relationship between me and Nicky. It also meant that when the horse ran next time there would be no question about whether I should be in the saddle and it was very satisfying knowing he would be there for me the following season after his summer break.

The First National Bank Chase at Ascot, formerly the H&T Walker Chase, was chosen for his comeback and with 11st 10lb on his back it was a tough assignment. He led his rivals every inch of the way and was absolutely breathtaking, jumping his fences with ease and beating Couldn't Be Better as well as several other good horses. That was my second big win on him and he returned to Ascot for the Betterware Cup a month later for his first attempt at three miles, a fair guide as to whether we ought to be considering a bid for the Gold Cup.

He now had the reputation for being a very talented front-runner, but with Young Hustler in the field there was at least one rival who would take him on in front. He fought off that rival and all other challenges to win, going away from Dubacilla who later that season finished second to Master Oats in the Gold Cup.

The big race at Cheltenham was suddenly a real possibility and while he was beaten in his next outing, the Peter Marsh Chase at Haydock won by Earth Summit, the ground was horrendous, very heavy, and did not suit Raymylette. He jumped well and I was still full of hope that he could give a good account at Cheltenham but his days were numbered when he suffered an attack of colic in March. He died under general anaesthetic on the operating table as vets fought to save his life. The date was 14 March 1995, the first day of the Cheltenham Festival.

The autopsy uncovered the reason for his untimely end and explained why he had been so difficult to feed. Normal food, even grass, would run straight through him, so he had been kept going on a limited diet of bran and oats; the Governor would go out to him last thing at night and give him a bowl of food because he ate better when offered smaller quantities. Little did we know that his digestive system had been terribly damaged by worms as a young horse, which meant he had been digesting his food through his intestine and not his stomach, which had effectively been rotting away. He was only a young horse when he died and it is still sad to think what he might have achieved.

I arrived at the races feeling very low and fighting hard not to think how tough fate had been, when luck turned the corner again and I won the Ritz Chase on Rough Quest. How ironic that my second winner at the Festival should come on the day that my first winner died.

There have been several other horses who made getting up in the morning a pleasure. Amtrak Express, on whom I won the Agfa Diamond Chase at Sandown, is a lovely little horse, a Trojan, and while he lacks the talent of others, his general ability and attitude are wonderful. For want of a better phrase, he is everything that racing should be. Big Matt is another who has won decent races, he lacks a bit of class but is good enough to give his owners a lot of pleasure by competing at grade-one racecourses.

Having said I love horses, there are those I don't like riding. Their common trait is dishonesty. They don't or won't give their best when they race, and while it might not be their fault, the vices of unwilling individuals are a nightmare to solve. Good trainers and their staff can often overcome the problems to a degree and if I can help I will happily do so. Getting the best from a thoroughbred racehorse covers a multitude of issues, from feeding, training, schooling and fitness, to picking races on suitable ground and at the right track, through handicapping, the resting time between races and jockeyship. In that respect some trainers are way ahead of others, seemingly pulling all the strands together successfully on a regular basis.

How hard this regime should be is an issue over which there can be few rules. Horses come in too many shapes and sizes and with vastly differing constitutions to make any binding statements. Some trainers choose to run a horse as often as possible when it is in winning form, reasoning it is better to pick up every opportunity; others prefer to make less use of a winning horse in a bid to get good service over many seasons and they accept that some winning chances will just have to go begging.

Much will depend on the robustness and breeding of the horse. The Blue Boy, who had spells with Martin Pipe, Jackie Retter and Peter Bowen, stands out as one who coped with a prodigious amount of racing and rewarded his owners with numerous victories. He suffered a broken shoulder at Taunton fairly late in his career, a sad end but one which showed how fate can strike at any moment and why some trainers believe in taking winning chances when they can. There is no guarantee of avoiding injury just because a horse has been wrapped in cotton-wool.

Other horses will definitely not benefit from such strenuous lives and the signs will be obvious to any reasonable trainer. In racing we often talk about horses finding the experience of going to the course 'blows their minds'; they simply get too excited and exhausted by the journey, the crowd, other horses and the exertions of the race. Weight falls off them after such an experience and it takes time to put back on because they often pick at their food for days after a race. Such horses simply cannot be raced too frequently and are almost bound to fail if the signs are ignored.

One occasion when it is tempting to go for another quick run is when a horse is reassessed by the handicapper and therefore has to carry more weight in future races. Since that new weight does not take immediate effect it is tempting to run the horse before its new handicap mark takes effect, a ploy which can work well if the horse is tough enough to cope with plenty of racing. There are no hard rules, trainers have to decide what suits individual horses, and since some owners like going to the races a lot while others prefer to wait patiently for the right opportunity, sensible trainers do their best to put the right horse with the right owner, otherwise any amount of disagreement can fester.

Of two things I'm sure: some horses should not be in training and some trainers should not be in racing. Admittedly, it is not always possible to tell a horse's ability until it has tackled a few races, but some are blatantly hopeless yet are seen running time and again. Worse, is the sight of horses at the races that are ill-prepared by people who shouldn't be in the industry. All these horses are ever going to do is get a jockey hurt and burn holes in an owner's pocket and an owner may be lost to racing for good. It is an area in which the Jockey Club must tighten up. Naive owners are being ripped off and what is tantamount to horse abuse, while rare in racing, must be stamped out.

The horse is a very strong animal, however, and it would be nice if a few rogues could be asked to give up jockey abuse! Okay, we have the choice about riding in races and the horse, in theory, doesn't (although they do refuse to race if that's their wish). Jockey abuse concerns those horses which would scare the pants off any horseman, and while I've been lucky enough to avoid too many dangerous incidents, one – at Bellewstown when I was 15 – will always be remembered as a complete nightmare.

Cantering to the post for a five-furlong sprint, the horse I was riding suddenly took off. With his head in the air the metal bit in his mouth was rendered useless and I was left hanging on, a passenger on a runaway who seemed unsure about either his destination or mine. Ahead were the starting stalls, placed in the centre of the track, and now looming into view. If we had hit them at that speed I would have ended up looking like a piece of cheese that's been pressed through a grater. Fear awoke some inner sense in me and, pointing him towards a gap no wider than an armchair between the running rails and the stalls, we flashed through, miraculously avoiding stalls handlers and the other horses gathering at the start.

My relief was sweet but brief as ahead lay nothing but post and rail fencing. 'I'm dead,' I thought. 'I'm dead.' The horse seemed to wake up to this fact too, recognising that if I was going to die, he was coming with me. Jamming on his brakes was too little, too late and, slithering towards a concrete upright, he suddenly leapt in the air, throwing me into orbit at the same time.

Falling off was never such a relief, before or since. Breathless I lay there, glad of the sky above and the grass swathed around me. I took this as a sign that I was still on earth and not waiting outside the gates of heaven.

That was the scariest ride I have had on a horse, and while I am more experienced and stronger now there are still occasions when I think to myself, 'I'm not in control here', and that's not a nice feeling. I can't say it's frightening, but it is grim. There is also the occasion when something completely out of the blue happens, something you don't expect – it's generally over before you've had time to think of the consequences, but I suppose such occasions can be pretty shocking afterwards and do end in injuries when your luck is out.

I rode a novice chaser for Ron Hodges many years ago who performed a suicidal act for no reason. In the paddock before the race Ron said: 'This fella jumps really well and he's been placed in point-to-points. Bounce him out in the first four.'

'Okay,' I said, and, when the tapes went up, I made sure I was in the right place and galloping towards the first fence. We met it on what seemed a perfect stride but my partner inexplicably kept galloping instead of jumping and he parted the birch literally at the roots of the fence. In most cases this would send a horse cartwheeling, the deceleration causing the back legs to come past the front, but incredibly he stayed on his feet and I kept my balance in the saddle. I remember thinking, 'That was not very clever, what the hell is going on in his head?' Since horses are not thick, I reasoned he would make a better job of the second fence. It's still hard to believe he could try the same stunt, or perhaps he had something wrong, but again he made no attempt to jump and this time turned over good and proper. I was lucky, I shook myself down and walked away. Horses can be unpredictable, that is for sure.

IV

Trainers, Owners and Agents

Until a few years ago jockeys' agents were unheard of and most riders were committed to one or two trainers by being their 'stable jockey'. All the top riders were associated with a yard in that way and all young jockeys dreamt of getting an agreement with one of the top trainers – anything else would have been unthinkable.

As stable jockey to Nicky Henderson I was following a tradition which had worked well for several centuries. For a while I was also number two jockey to Henrietta Knight at Wantage, a situation in which Nicky had first call on me but I would ride for Henrietta whenever possible. As her yard expanded, there was a need for someone who was more readily available and we ended our agreement on good terms a couple of seasons ago, although I still enjoy riding her horses when the opportunity arises.

While the retained-jockey system still operates and many big yards or owners have contracts with riders, its importance is being slightly eroded through a number of evolutionary changes. One crucial difference between now and 20 years ago is the emergence of agents who work for jockeys and book their rides in races. In my case that means topping up the rides I am guaranteed for the Henderson stable; if the boss does not have a runner in a race, my agent tries to ensure I get one.

Jockeys have all sorts of agreements with various people but most work with a full-time agent to obtain rides. The former champion Richard Dunwoody, who some would call the premier rider of the nineties, was stable jockey to the prolific Martin Pipe stable, then became a freelance in Britain with an agreement to ride horses trained by Dermot Weld in Ireland, then gained a retainer with the wealthy owner Robert Ogden whose horses are trained at a number of stables around Britain. Flexibility is a key requirement from trainers and jockeys and there is no better example of that than at Martin Pipe's yard, which has no official number one jockey but uses Tony McCoy on a 'when available' basis through consultation with his agent. Undoubtedly, the agent has been the catalyst for much change and some would say a good agent is now more important to a jockey than a good stable. I still put huge faith and value in the retainer I enjoy with Nicky, but equally I would say that any jockey who does not have someone booking their rides is getting left behind, particularly where big races are concerned.

Good agents get rides for their jockeys in all sorts of ways. They establish successful relationships with trainers, which is probably the first requirement, and they also have an instinctive feeling for opportunities that are going begging. They seem to know when a jockey is about to be suspended or injured before the rider knows themselves, and are there to snap up the spare rides as soon as they are available – that might be mercenary to some, but it is good business practice to others.

Getting in at the start of a venture which is about to take off can be down to great foresight or pure luck. In my case forming an association with Dave Roberts was simply a case of picking up the phone and saying, 'I need someone to book my rides, will you do it for me?' That was in 1992, I was 22 and still a conditional jockey living in Devon and working for Jackie Retter. A few winners were coming my way and some nice things were being said about my ability but I was hardly the sort of jockey who could instantly add riches to Dave's bank account. That did not seem to worry him. He replied 'yes' in that phone call and I know I have had no cause for regrets.

Dave, who lives at Redhill in Surrey, has since become the best-known and most successful jockeys' agent in the country, handling rides for many of Britain's top riders, including Tony McCoy, Norman Williamson, Richard Johnson and Adrian Maguire. He is asked to take on more jockeys than he can handle, with requests coming in each year from aspiring youngsters and older, established riders and he accommodates a new face or two each year as members of his 'stable' move on or retire.

Top people in their field are very close to the action, and that is definitely true in Dave's case. Prerequisites for his job include knowing the right people, knowing what is about to happen, having a knowledge of the form book and being a 'race reader', which means having the ability to analyse races in order to spot the strengths and weaknesses of horses. He does go racing, but rarely, and most of his analysis is gleaned by watching the satellite television service the Racing Channel. He knows exactly which horses to avoid and which ones he would like to get his jockeys on and he misses very little.

Successful people always have their detractors and Dave is no different. He has perfected the art of booking rides for jockeys and, since anything new in racing has to overcome centuries of tradition, he has had his share of criticism. I've heard jockeys who are not under his wing accuse him of stealing rides, but I defend him by saying he is simply doing his job. He will not ring a trainer to book a ride for one of his jockeys if he knows someone else is established on that horse, although sometimes that is not always clear. For instance, a trainer may have used several jockeys on a horse and the most recent one may feel they have an agreement to continue the partnership, but until that is made clear Dave is justified in making a bid for the ride. Another example might be if a rider looks like having two options in a race, or being booked to ride at two meetings. Dave will step in then and try to secure the rides that the jockey cannot take, and if it looks like he is treading on toes it is not intentional, he is simply ensuring that his jockeys receive maximum opportunities.

One reason why Dave is successful is because he gets on very well with trainers, which in my case means working alongside my boss Nicky Henderson, who is based at a yard known as Seven Barrows just outside Lambourn in Berkshire. He trains 100 horses and pays me a retainer to ride for his stable. Dave and Nicky respect each other and work together to ensure they get the best use of my services. That might mean Nicky telling Dave that a horse he has entered for a future race is unlikely to run, allowing Dave the opportunity to cast around for a suitable spare ride for me. In return, there is a benefit to Nicky when planning ahead, in that Dave can tell him which of his jockeys is already booked. That gives the Governor an insight into which horses are likely to be running in a race.

Another advantage of riding for the best and most prolific agent is that if I have to turn a ride down, Dave can offer another very good alternative, which keeps him popular with owners and trainers and, in turn, benefits all his jockeys.

I'm very lucky to ride for Nicky Henderson. He is one of the premier trainers in Britain and also a friend. Racing fans will know him as a man who has constantly been a player on the big stage, and while there has not been a champion in the yard in the past year or two I am convinced the glory days will return to Seven Barrows before long. Those past successes include the fantastic achievement of coaxing three Champion Hurdle victories from See You Then – a rare feat and particularly meritorious because of the horse's fragility.

In any sport success fluctuates and in racing that means a yard is picking up major prizes one moment and missing out the next. Such success is all relative – a very small yard with two horses can win a Gold Cup during a season in which it might not win another race, while a big yard can achieve 60 winners but still feel disappointed to have failed on the big occasion. Luck can play a very big part: a horse can go lame on the eve of a championship, or it can be brought down by another horse which falls in the race, or it can simply make a blunder at the last jump and be narrowly beaten. Many yards have enjoyed quite fantastic periods when they have housed a number of champions at the same time, only to find them difficult to replace when they reach retirement. That has certainly been the case for British trainers in recent years, particularly when they have gone shopping for bloodstock in Ireland, a wonderful source of young horses until the Irish economy boomed and an increasing number were kept to race in their own country. That does not mean horses are not on the market but they do not always turn out to be as useful as their pedigree and appearance suggested and, once again, a trainer can have no end of bad luck in that regard. Worse still, when things are not going well the best horses seem to get injured or simply lose their form, and veterinary science cannot explain why. On top of the usual knocks which all thoroughbreds receive there is also 'the virus', a general term for a range of ailments which afflict horses, causing them to cough or go off their feed, or simply look unwell. In some cases, horses will show no sign of illness, their coats shine, they gallop with enthusiasm at home but they fail to produce any sparkle when asked to make an effort in a race. It is like driving a car which develops a fault and then produces only half the power.

As a jockey much of my work is done by 'feel' which I use to assess the way a horse likes to be ridden and the ground, track and type of race which would suit it; information which I can pass on to the horse's owner and trainer. Riding a virus-stricken victim negates the role I play.

Like the common cold, viruses are part of life now, and while I don't believe Lambourn has a particular problem the large population of horses stabled in the vicinity means there are bound to be a lot of reported cases. Seven Barrows is about three miles out of Lambourn and better placed to avoid cross-infection between horses, but in common with just about every yard in the country it has had its problems.

In the autumn of 1997 the horses went down with a bug and the Governor immediately put the whole string on the easy list. Two weeks of walking and trotting was pretty boring for the staff but it gave the horses a chance to put all their strength into shaking off the ailment. That paid dividends when we returned to the racetrack – and for one golden period just about every horse won or performed better than expected.

Trainers and owners have to show patience when such a virus hits a yard and they also have to be vigilant and take precautions. When a new horse arrives at Seven Barrows it is put in a stable away from the other horses for a short period to see whether it shows any symptoms of illness; stables are regularly disinfected, the lorry which transports the horses gets hosed clean with disinfectant after every journey and all horses at the yard have their temperatures taken twice a day.

Businesses have to accept knocks, but the good ones survive because the foundations are solid, and that is certainly the case at Seven Barrows where Nicky and his wife Diana's hard work and talent have built a base of loyal owners. He is a fantastic 'people-person' and has a wonderful rapport with his owners who consequently stick with him. From my perspective, as stable jockey, it is simply a pleasure to be dealing with a gentleman who attracts similar customers.

Those customers, the owners, have the prerogative to move their horses when and where they choose, but if the Governor is ever asked to take a horse which is with another trainer he will always phone them to have a few words – he knows the disappointment such a decision can bring since it has happened to him, and rather than just send a lorry round to collect the horse he does his best to ensure the change-over is done as painlessly as possible.

His strengths include being a good judge of races, which is a very important attribute and which makes my life easier when horses are beaten since I know he is not going to be flapping and getting heated, as he can see the evidence and the reason for the defeat. He was given a good insight into the difficulties faced by jockeys through his own time as an amateur rider while working as an assistant to the great Lambourn trainer Fred Winter. While there he won the Imperial Cup on Acquaint in 1977 and rode in the Grand National and at the Cheltenham Festival.

My association with him began after I had become champion conditional jockey in the 1992–93 season, having ridden 54 winners. As a conditional rider you can claim a weight allowance in races – 7lb until winning 15 races, 5lb until winning 30 races and 3lb until winning 55 races. If a jockey begins the season as a conditional but passes the point at which they can claim an allowance, they remain classified in the novice category until the end of that season.

Winning the title was a useful bit of publicity and the 54 winners meant I had been in the public eye a fair bit, so the chances of a job offer from a big stable were as good as at any time in my career. Rumours spread like forest fires when it comes to jobs in racing, and while changes don't attract quite the publicity given to the annual musical chairs in Formula One motor racing, there was a fair bit of interest in the summer of 1993 because several top stables and their jockeys seemed to be going in different directions.

The domino effect had been started, unwittingly, by the great

Peter Scudamore who had chosen to retire, leaving vacant the much-vaunted job at Martin Pipe's stable. Irish champion jockey Charlie Swan was among those said to be in the frame but it was Richard Dunwoody who eventually moved to Nicholashayne, and since he had been riding for Nicky's stable a vacancy was suddenly open at Seven Barrows.

At that time I was working with and riding for Jackie Retter at her yard near Exeter, and quite happy with the deal, of which more later. Yet as an ambitious man in his early twenties, talk of big stables looking for jockeys was more than just a little interesting. I was at a successful, medium-sized yard with some 20 horses, while a big stable would have four or five times that number. That brings added pressure to a jockey, but it was also just the sort of challenge I was seeking. When I met Nicky at Ascot Sales and he asked me to pay him a visit 'for a chat' I knew we weren't going to be talking about the price of Guinness.

I also knew I was not the only jockey with whom he had been in discussion about the job. Charlie Swan had been one possibility and Norman Williamson, 18 months older than me and better established in the pecking order, had been first choice. It transpired that he rejected the offer after being told that Dunwoody and Jamie Osborne would retain one or two choice rides on horses they had already ridden, such as Remittance Man and Travado. Norman chose instead to join Kim Bailey, a decision which reached a zenith two years later when Alderbrook and Master Oats won the Champion Hurdle–Gold Cup double.

The offer Nicky put to me was the same as for Norman, and while it would have been nice to hear him say that I would ride all the horses, I knew that would be unrealistic when Dunwoody had forged a winning partnership with Remittance Man, the best horse in the yard at that time. I would have to be patient and I knew it, but I felt it would be weak of me not to stress that I had no desire to be second fiddle. The Governor, as Nicky is known to all the staff at the yard, responded by saying it would not be like that. 'As far as I'm concerned, if we both get on together you will ride all the horses in the yard one day,' he said, and he later proved as good as his word.

I felt sure this should be my next move but I was also fully aware of the debt I owed Jackie, and asked for time to consider the offer – a sensible move I felt, even though I was so chuffed by events I tingled and had to stop in a lay-by soon after I left Seven Barrows to reflect on what had been a momentous few hours in my life.

Not surprisingly it was a wrench to leave Jackie's yard, but I had to take up the offer in Lambourn and have never regretted the decision. Joining a big yard added to my standing in racing and meant I was a more likely candidate for decent spare rides when they became available. But, more important than that, I have been able to share some really rewarding days with the trainer and staff at Seven Barrows. It is a team effort which gets horses to the races in peak condition and being part of that team gives me a buzz and certainly makes up for days when things go wrong.

In that respect the Governor is a very fair man to work for and in six years, and after sitting on about 1,000 runners from the yard, he has given me a roasting on only two occasions. That either suggests I make few errors or he is generously tight-lipped but either way I am not complaining. One thing is sure, all jockeys make mistakes, most trainers let them know, so to aspiring riders I say, be prepared. Getting told you made a mistake is never particularly pleasant no matter what the situation, but where the Governor is concerned the issue never rankles – he says what he thinks and then presses on with the business of producing winners. One such occasion came after I rode Billy Bathgate in the Grand Annual Chase at the Cheltenham Festival.

A useful horse on his day, Billy Bathgate suffered from wind problems. A wind problem for a horse is the same as a breathing problem for a human but since the thoroughbred needs maximum air-flow when racing, any fault in the breathing mechanism can ruin their chances of a successful career. Such problems can be cured but they are often the bane of a trainer's life. Horses which suffer from wind trouble often need individual attention – they may be particularly susceptible to dust and need to be turned out into a paddock each day, their hay and bedding requirements may be different from other horses, they may need to race with their tongues tied down with a strap or with a tube inserted into their necks, allowing maximum airflow into the lungs when there is a blockage in the throat. Most need to avoid very heavy, testing ground, since that requires more effort and deeper breaths – finding good ground for them to race on and relying on their natural speed is sometimes the only way of conjuring a victory.

I asked the vet James Main, who looks after the string at Seven Barrows, to summarise wind problems and his first reaction was to say: 'Have you got two hours?' He did add, however, that problems in the larynx (part of the tube in the throat which carries air to and from the lungs) the soft palate (which sits under the larynx and can dislocate when a horse gallops blocking air-flow) and disease in the upper and lower airway are just some of the reasons why horses choke and splutter when attempting to draw in lungfuls of air. Larynx failure can range from weakness of movement to paralysis on one side which restricts the amount of oxygen reaching the lungs.

Research into wind problems continues, as it does with that other well-known thoroughbred affliction, breaking blood vessels, which can be a subsidiary effect of breathing difficulties. The sight of blood trickling down a horse's nose after it has been galloping is often the first sign that a blood vessel has broken and, while horses can be cured of this unpleasant affliction, serious cases may have to be retired.

Racegoers and punters are often unaware of these problems which can make it difficult for them to back horses and, since their confidence in the sport is vital, steps are being made to give them more information, particularly if a horse runs badly for no reason. The *Racing Post* now carries a weekly column which details information given to the Jockey Club by trainers of horses which ran badly. This often reveals that a horse has broken a blood vessel or 'gurgled', a noise which sounds like its name and denotes breathing deficiencies.

There are any number of problems for jockeys when riding such horses as they may have to be nursed through their races, given plenty of time to recover when they make a mistake at a jump and may need a period in a race when they are allowed to coast along in order to get a second wind. None of this may be apparent to the punter or the press and while they may look on and assume a jockey has not given them much of a run for their money, it can be that the person in the saddle has little option but to give the horse a sympathetic ride.

Billy Bathgate was just such a horse, and while I was naturally very glad to be riding him at the Festival it is not a venue where you want to be battling against the odds – the competition is white-hot and each participant is right in the spotlight.

On that occasion there were 20 runners and so I wanted to be handy, in a position near the front where I could counter any moves by the leaders and without the need to come around a wall of horses – about sixth or seventh would have suited me fine.

Billy Bathgate was a genuine horse, not prone to digging his toes in, but to add to my difficulties he 'planted' himself at the starting gate. Maybe it was the big occasion, the sights and sounds of Cheltenham during Festival week being many times more colourful and loud than a typical day at any other track, but his mind was elsewhere as the starter called us in and he hesitated, looked up and stood still. For some horses that means nothing on earth will shift them until the race is off and they can return to their stables – and there have been some very famous rogues like that in racing down the years.

On this occasion Billy Bathgate was always going to join in, but his temporary pause meant the other runners swarmed past us and formed a line in front of the tape and my good position near the front was now a very bad one at the back. No doubt you have all seen similar incidents when watching televised races and heard a consternated jockey shout, 'no sir, no sir', in a bid to prevent the starter letting the field go until they have recovered some of the ground, pushing their horse in between tightly squeezed rivals, or being forced to trot along the backs of the horses to get some daylight on the outside of the field.

I managed to get Billy Bathgate into something like the right place, but soon after we had begun racing he started 'choking', a gurgling-type noise which told me he was having trouble breathing. I knew I had to give him time to recover, to ease off him so that he could relax a little and clear his windpipe, but I also knew that in this particular race, run over the minimum distance of two miles, there was not going to be much time in which to take a breather.

The form book comment of the race revealed: 'Slowly into stride: ran on from two out: never nearer.' Punters might have seen it another way and said, 'Well behind and given no chance of a decent position, finished like a train, given far too much to do by jockey.' Like I say, it is not always easy for those in the grandstand to appreciate the difficulties, but cheating is not part of my repertoire. We finished fifth and seemed to fly up the hill, but only because every other horse in the race was stopping through tiredness and Billy Bathgate had been coasting for much of the race.

The look on the boss's face said plenty as I returned towards the unsaddling area. He looked at me and let rip: 'That's crazy, there is no way a horse can win from that position at this meeting. It's an absolute disgrace.' He was right, and while I could have made excuses I had to acknowledge that it didn't look good and that I had to take some of the blame for the poor start.

I had to simply swallow my pride and quickly hurried back to the weighing-room ready for a ride in the next race. You will appreciate that while there wasn't much time for dwelling on the Billy Bathgate ride I did feel awkward when I faced the Governor to hand him my saddle but he immediately put me at my ease. The mist had cleared, the incident had been forgotten and he was now focused on the next event, something I always admire about him.

'Right, you know this horse,' he said, filling me with confidence, even though it was to be the first time I had sat on him in public. 'Go out there and give him a really good ride.' And because life is so rich in diversity, and because the horse in question was the super Raymylette, I was about to ride my first Cheltenham Festival winner.

The other occasion I felt humbled and red-faced by the Governor's reaction was after I rode in a novice hurdle at Taunton on a horse called Garnwin who was having his first run. He was very green and seemed most unsure about what was happening around him and, as luck would have it, I had to run wide of several horses on the last bend in a bid to get a clear passage towards the final two hurdles. We were beaten just over a length by a runner from Philip Hobbs' yard called Lucky Eddie.

If I remember correctly, the Governor's words included such phrases as 'gone round the world on him' and 'thrown away any chances of winning', which were both correct, even though I was bursting with ifs and buts about the way the race had unfolded. I limited it to saying that Garnwin had not been racing like a potential winner until the home turn. When I pulled him wide of the other horses he began to stretch and race with more confidence, but I was not to know in advance that this would happen as the horse was having his first outing in a race. However, the boss's words were based on facts which could not be denied, so, as neither of us wanted to turn the event into an issue, we simply discussed the horse in greater detail when he next ran, an example of team effort. You must be able to give a trainer an honest opinion of their horse and not merely tell them what they would like to hear. Masking the truth could jeopardise future chances of winning a race – if you are honest you can constructively work out what makes a horse tick.

Successful trainers are consistently near the top of the table for winners and prize-money won and Nicky Henderson fits into that category, yet when it comes to breaking records there is no one to match Martin Pipe, who is based on the Devon–Somerset border near Wellington.

In conjunction with the seven-time champion jockey Peter Scudamore, Pipe turned the business of training jumpers upside-down and while many people have copied his methods he still seems to keep ahead of the competition. His success breeds success and encourages owners to send him horses so his early hard work should pay off for years to come, but he still seeks new boundaries. One recent example of this has been his buying of French-bred five-year-olds who are very mature yet get weight allowances in races from older horses. The rules might be changed one day to remove this advantage but it is typical of Pipe that he should make use of it while he can.

Until Pipe came along, tearaway horses made the running in

races, the decent horses galloped in the middle and the no-hopers stayed at the rear. Pipe worked out that if he could get horses ultra-fit and well schooled they could make the running and hold an advantage which would be difficult to claw back. This has directly affected the way races have been run in the nineties and most contests now have a sharp pace from the start, which in turn has made jockeys develop a keener sense of awareness when they come into line at the tapes. No longer can a jockey on a hot favourite assume they can dawdle at the start and pick off their rivals at will.

Much has been made of Pipe's method of interval training in which he gives horses several short canters on an all-weather gallop. This certainly made many trainers reassess their own methods and I know that when his autobiography was published it became vital reading, even though many people discovered that what they were doing was little different from the master. The book certainly opened up Pipe's world to a public eager to know why he was so successful. This had led to rumours about wonder drugs and various other potions which gave his horses an edge. He was also hauled into the mire by a programme involving the investigative reporter Roger Cook which said he was cruel to his horses. That failed to produce any evidence and, while potentially damaging, Pipe simply trained more winners and the matter was quickly forgotten.

Quick-thinking and apparently always in a hurry, his character has been the subject of many profiles. When Richard Dunwoody and David Bridgwater quit as his stable jockeys after brief spells at the yard, people asked whether the trainer had become impossible to work for and too demanding, a suggestion accentuated by the long association he had previously enjoyed with Scudamore.

He now uses Tony McCoy on a freelance basis and, while training hundreds of winners every season, still has his critics. I have heard it said that he runs horses too often, yet if a horse wins eight moderate races it is probably taking less out of itself than if it is slogging hard against tougher competition. Pipe's ability to improve horses, as well as his eye for those precocious, tough types who handle the firm ground which keeps many rivals in their stables, are other factors in his success. If his owners are happy, who can blame him for taking the chances that come his way? My own involvement with Pipe has been limited to a few winners, a runner-up spot in the Welsh Champion Hurdle on Daraydan and unplaced efforts in the Champion Hurdle on Granville Again and Cadougold, but I hope to be associated with him many more times in the future.

The only person to prise the trainer's championship from Pipe in recent years is David Nicholson. Known as 'The Duke', Nicholson is one of the most respected men in the business and while he appears unapproachable on occasions that aura hides a very good-hearted person and an amusing one too. His record as a trainer speaks for itself but he also deserves to be recognised for coaching young jockeys, a talent he inherited from his father, 'Frenchie', whose most celebrated success was in grooming Pat Eddery, the former champion flat jockey. Peter Scudamore made his name while riding for The Duke who was himself a top rider in the sixties and seventies, and Adrian Maguire and Richard Johnson have been honed into top-class acts while at the yard. There was a fair bit of controversy surrounding The Duke and his employer, Colin Smith, during Christmas 1998 when Maguire resigned as stable jockey amid press speculation that Johnson, who was his deputy, would be promoted to number one. This was denied, but Maguire felt his position untenable – although he continued riding winners for the yard as a freelance. The press also said The Duke would retire at the end of the season, but I suspect he will be around for a few years yet. He is not the type of man to appreciate being shoved out of a job and the more people speculate about his retirement the more he will laugh at the rumours.

I have met and got to know numerous trainers over the years – those who helped me through my early career I have discussed in a separate chapter – and I have the greatest respect for many in the profession. They work in a job which offers great rewards but the slog to produce the best involves seven days each week and long hours in each of those days. The disappointment when a good horse goes wrong is unbearable on occasions. With that in mind I must mention Tim Forster, who retired from training in 1998 but was a wonderful man to ride for because he took defeat and bad circumstance on the chin and waved it away.

Quite simply he was a great loser, a fine quality because there is so much losing to be done in this game. In contrast, some trainers and owners get huffy on occasions and that is hard for a jockey who has done his best. I always try to accept that attitude, knowing there is a lot at stake even in quite small races and it is natural for people to show their disappointment.

John O'Shea, who I have ridden for since my earliest days as a jockey striving to make the grade, is another in the Forster mould, being a gentleman who accepts defeat and enjoys victory. He does a fine job with his horses – as does Noel Chance, who struggled to make a living in Ireland before moving to Lambourn but whose Gold Cup win with Mr Mulligan showed what he can do when given the right material. I have ridden a good few winners for Noel and also for Jim Old, whose career pinnacle to date must be the Champion Hurdle victory of Collier Bay, a horse who could yet make a very good chaser. Jim is great company on and off the racecourse, as I have found when we play golf together. He had a lean spell in his training career at the end of the eighties and early in the nineties, but he kept plugging on and has now got a very good yard, some quality horses and some loyal owners, notably Wally Sturt who owns Collier Bay.

My brother-in-law Paul Nicholls (his wife Bridget is sister of my wife Jane) definitely deserves a mention at this point. He has done fantastically well, starting his training career from scratch after quitting as a jockey and making the most of his strengths to become another leading player in jump-racing. Through hard work he and Bridget have put together a really good team and while their association with Paul Barber, who owns their yard and gallops, has been crucial, no one can deny they have done a first-rate job in attracting owners and getting the best from their horses. Victories in the Scottish National with Belmont King and King George VI Chase with See More Business have placed Paul at the top of his profession. He is very ambitious and has probably trodden on a few toes when acquiring horses to train, but more often than not that is because he has been asked to take a horse by an owner who has spotted his talent.

At one point, when Paul was getting going, I rode most of his horses and when he expanded I was offered the job of stable jockey on two occasions. However, I was already committed to

Nicky Henderson and could not do both jobs, although I still ride for Paul when it suits us both.

Philip Hobbs, Somerset-based like Paul, is another trainer whom I hold in very high regard and whom I particularly like riding for. He is very analytical after races and never fails to ask questions, which I enjoy because that shows he is looking to gain an extra length or two improvement from his horses. One thing that infuriates me is when I give an opinion to a trainer on a horse I have ridden, perhaps suggesting blinkers or a longer trip or firmer ground would suit, and that advice is ignored. I always try to give an honest opinion and with Philip you always feel he is taking your thoughts on board for serious consideration.

Henrietta Knight is a pleasure to ride for and I remember the impression left on me when I began exercising her horses soon after arriving in Lambourn. After spending so much of my time booting around the West Country it felt like a liberty to be sitting on horses which were that little bit better and so well schooled and balanced. A good horse in a bad race gallops effortlessly, and riding Henrietta's horses, whether on the racecourse or while doing work at home, always left me feeling there was untapped potential.

Perhaps racing's most famous trainer is Jenny Pitman, dubbed 'The Queen of Aintree' for her two victories in the Grand National. She also has strong views about the course and happily makes them known if asked. Mrs P., as the jockeys know her, is very much her own woman with her own ideas and there has certainly never been a man nor printed word which could change her mind, although her son Mark, who was number one jockey at her Lambourn yard for several seasons, probably had as much influence as any before he retired. Trying to tell Mrs P. something with which she disagrees merely annoys her and while many big-race victories speak for her talents as a trainer she never asked for my opinion again after one occasion when I was asked to take part in a schooling session.

At Seven Barrows we school novices by cantering them steadily towards the fence or hurdle before asking them to quicken several strides from it. This gives plenty of impulsion for a fast jump and exit away from the fence but also allows you to judge your take-off point pretty accurately to ensure you are neither too close nor too far from the obstacle. Horses that are quick over their jumps can take lengths off their rivals, which is what racing is all about. Without asking too many questions this was how I assumed Mrs P. would want her young horses taught when I arrived at her yard a couple of years ago in company with Graham Bradley when we had been asked to go there to school some novice chasers.

We duly got mounted, rode up to the gallops and jumped in tandem over a series of three little fences. My horse was a bit keen underneath me, which meant I had to work to steady him, quite natural with a young horse, but I was pleased with the final outcome when he winged the fences and had no doubt Mrs P., who had been surveying the session on foot, would be equally satisfied.

'That was very good,' I said, as we drew alongside.

'Good!' said Mrs P. with an air of astonishment. 'If he does that on the bloody racecourse he'll end up sitting in a lump on the far side of it! I don't want my horses jumping like that. You get hold of that horse and you get him balanced all the way into the fence and all the way out of it.'

Like I said earlier, you don't argue with Mrs P. so I did as I was told and jumped the fences as she instructed, although the horse did not jump anywhere near as well. 'There,' she said, when we trotted back towards her: 'That was much better.'

Brad and I were not the only people to get a bollocking that morning. Mrs P.'s son, Mark, also slipped up. After admonishing us for the way we had jumped the horses, she turned to Mark, who had only recently retired from race-riding and said, 'Have you got your helmet?'

'No,' replied Mark innocently.

The thunder cloud descended over the great lady's head again. 'I told you to bring your helmet in case you had to show these jockeys how to ride,' she remonstrated.

She was not joking either, and Mark looked sheepish, knowing Brad and I, his recent colleagues, would not be impressed at the suggestion.

Racing relies on groups of people, all vital, although it is often said that owners are the most important. Without the horses there could be no racing and if stable staff or jockeys and trainers went on strike it would be difficult to see how it could continue, but the owners have to be the starting point. I accept that breeders, who supply the raw material, might question that view. Ultimately, every spoke in the wheel is essential but while most of us make at least some money from the industry, owners have to be encouraged to come back year in, year out, knowing they are likely to lose money. It is the same with any hobby, but racing does not come cheap.

Being made to feel welcome by the owners at Seven Barrows was a great relief and it certainly helped when I first joined the yard. I have got to know some of them quite well since and while I rarely see them away from the races it is nice to share a drink with them when we have a winner. There is not always a lot of time, and since I often have a long journey to make followed by an early start the next day it is not always convenient to stay behind after racing. I certainly never feel obliged to share a drink with an owner, but it is often a lot of fun to share their joy and join in when I have made a contribution.

My role is simply to produce the best from their horses, and while we have been to a few parties with owners down the years I certainly don't spend my spare time borrowing their yachts or flying in private jets to tropical islands. Lynn Wilson, owner of horses such as Barna Boy and Who's Equiname, is chairman of Northamptonshire Cricket Club and has offered me tickets to watch some matches there, while Michael Buckley and Anthony Speelman are both members of Sunningdale Golf Club and have invited me to take my clubs to the course, but it would be wrong to assume a jump-jockey socialises among the rich and famous.

One very welcome aspect of being associated with Nicky Henderson's stable is that I get to ride for jump-racing's most famous and respected owner, the Queen Mother, who generally has about five horses in training at the yard. When I ride one of her horses I am always left with the impression that she takes a passionate interest in its well-being and has a thorough knowledge of racing in general. I also find myself caught up in what might be termed 'the feel-good factor' which seems to envelop the Royal Family – they always seem to leave you feeling special about yourself, and I really cannot explain why.

It would be a privilege for most jockeys to ride for the Queen Mother and, while being an Irishman might suggest it would mean less to me, I have always had a great respect for Britain's Royal Family and am grateful for their interest in racing. In addition, the Queen Mother has owned so many famous horses down the years and employed so many legendary jockeys that I could not help but want to be a part, no matter how small, of that lineage. Speak to anyone who has pulled on Her Majesty's famous pale blue and gold colours, whether once or 100 times, and you will find a person with a sense of satisfaction. I remember chatting to David Mould, associated with so many of her winners, and noticing that he stepped up a gear when talking about those happy times.

I felt the same way after I had finally gained the opportunity, although I felt I was fated not to for a while after my first three attempts were dashed when racing was abandoned because of bad weather.

My first winner for her was Magic Junction at Ludlow, a meeting she was unable to attend and she was also absent when I gained a more significant victory in her colours on Cuddy Dale at Sandown Park in Esher, one of her favourite tracks and certainly one of my best memories. Cuddy Dale was a horse she had leased to run later in the season in the Grand Military Gold Cup and he was a most professional athlete with a bit of speed between jumps, absolutely at home around Sandown's demanding circuit where the Railway fences come in a group and really sort out good and bad jumpers. You can gain so many lengths if you are quick in and out of those fences and he really excelled in that respect. I remember thinking that the soldier who rode him in the Grand Military was going to be an extremely jammy bloke and while Cuddy Dale eventually finished only second to Act The Wag he again jumped for fun.

Riding Easter Ross to win at Windsor will stick in my memory since it was the first time I won for Her Majesty when she was in attendance. You don't need to be a brain surgeon to work out how to conduct yourself when introduced to a member of the Royal Family and, as her jockey, I bowed when meeting her in the paddock and had removed my gloves in case she offered to shake my hand, which she did. She then asked me some questions about Easter Ross, who was having his first run over hurdles, and when the bell rang to inform the jockeys to get mounted she said, 'Good luck. Let the horse enjoy himself.'

Making one of her first public appearances following an operation to replace a hip, the Queen Mother received warm applause from the crowd before the race and the reception in the winner's enclosure when we won was something to treasure. The joy on Her Majesty's face was unmistakable and when I dismounted and tried to explain to her how the race had unfolded I could barely speak for excitement.

I hardly know the Queen Mother but I honestly believe that despite being well into her nineties her mind is as sharp today as it was 30 or 40 years ago. That much is definitely true when it comes to racing and despite the fact she has owned hundreds of horses she can still tell you about each horse she owns today, young and old. Her involvement with racing is a fantastic advertisement for the sport, and in return I believe she gets many hours of pleasure following racing on television. Her Majesty either records or watches live every race in which her horses run. That gives me a special pleasure when I ride for her and I hope she remains fit and involved in racing for many years to come.

V

Injuries, Diet and Travel

You don't have to be a masochist to be a jump-jockey but physical self-punishment is part of the job. We wouldn't do it without the rewards, but by the time you take into account injuries, dieting and enough miles on the road to frighten a cabbie, this is no easy life.

Injuries are a grim aspect of the job, the sickening feeling when you know a bone has broken, the nausea which follows and the weeks or months of idleness are truly depressing. I try not to think about injuries but when you enter this profession you know you are going to get hurt – statistics show that jockeys take a fall once in every 14 rides – so you just hope you are one of the lucky ones who keeps the breakages to a minimum. Cases of concussion among jockeys average 40 over the past six seasons, although a new helmet with greater shock absorption is likely to reduce that figure, while fractures average 57, of which broken collar-bones account for 43 per cent. Over and above that, something which no one wants to contemplate, is the risk of being killed.

There have been many very sad cases of injuries to riders, but recently the two hardest to bear involved the death of Richard Davis following a fall at Southwell and the crippling injuries to Shane Broderick incurred at Fairyhouse. Richard's death in 1996 stunned racing and there was a gap in the weighing-room where he put his saddle and hung his clothes for many months. Time heals the general feeling of sadness but it never replaces people.

Most of my colleagues had to put the dangers raised by the tragedy to the back of their mind and get on with the job the following day but I had quite some time to reflect on the issue since I was on honeymoon in Sarasota and learnt the news when picking up a day-old copy of the *Daily Mail*. It was numbing to think of a fellow jockey being killed and very hard to be rational. A wave of emotions and jumbled questions go through your head at a time like that and while I never thought that this job's too dangerous and I'm quitting, and as far as I'm aware none of my colleagues did either, I suspect we all wondered whether the rides we take on horses who are liable to fall, through clumsiness or pig-headedness, are such a good idea. While no blame could be apportioned for Richard's death, and a Jockey Club investigation deemed that the horse involved, Mr Sox, had been properly prepared for the race, it made us aware that we must be careful about accepting rides before checking out their credentials. That is not easy when a spare ride suddenly becomes available halfway through a meeting, but it is worth deliberating for a second or two before saying yes. Even jockeys who are desperate for opportunities owe themselves that much, since they will certainly be sidelined if they get smashed up.

Turning rides down can be difficult and is generally done discreetly, but Carl Llewellyn became involved in a very public incident of this kind in 1997 when changing his mind about riding a horse for Malcolm Eckley. His volte-face came after a person whose view he respected said the horse was not a safe conveyance, but because Carl was declared as the jockey in the morning papers he suddenly found himself in a tight spot. That he stuck to his guns when many would have taken the easier option and ridden the horse is to his credit. With that doubt he could never have given the horse a fair ride, which would have been cheating the public, and he might well have been injured, a tough thing at the best of times, but far worse when you are lying there thinking: I could have avoided this. Connections of the horse were not best pleased, but it was, perhaps, a case of truth being stranger than fiction when substitute jockey Robert Bellamy was unseated at the first fence.

Turning down rides in that way does not mean a jockey has lost their nerve and while I frequently say no and forego the £84 riding fee, I have commitments to too many good owners, trainers and horses to risk getting crunched up unnecessarily.

On top of that I don't want to miss a big prize just because some bone-headed horse who has fallen on its two previous outings has gone for the hat-trick and buried me into the turf.

At least if a horse's form is very bad you can see it in writing, but all jockeys can tell of occasions when they have been put away by trainers who say a young horse, with little or no form, has been well schooled and has shown an aptitude for the job, only to find it is absolutely clueless in the race. You get to know which trainers to rely on when it comes to preparation of horses at home and which ones are less adept – perhaps they don't have the quality of staff, perhaps they think one jumping session over a few hurdles is adequate, or it could be that the horse has only been in their yard for a few weeks and has not yet betrayed its lunatic tendencies. Sometimes it seems they want the teaching to be done in a race, and while there is a rule which says horses must not be schooled on the course, the jockey can do precious little else if his partner has just barged its way through the first two fences. When you have gained experience you get to know what to expect, but you still do the best job you can and choose your words carefully after the race – the same trainer might have a smart little handicap hurdler who is a paragon of virtue and of course you don't want to jeopardise your chances of getting on his back, so you have to be diplomatic on occasions.

Shane's situation is very tough following a fall from a horse with the ironic name Another Deadly, which left him paralysed, this after he had ridden a winner in the previous race. He encapsulates those twin emotions – elation and despair – which most people experience in their lives but which jump-jockeys confront on a daily basis. Every ride could be our last but it could also lead to glory and riches. For Shane the glory peaked in his association with Doran's Pride, but that good horse apart, his career was blossoming. It ended in a second, the television pictures vividly portraying the seriousness of a fall which left him severely disabled.

As a jockey considering Shane's position I have to remain detached, knowing it could be me next time. My job depends on being 100 per cent committed to the business of racing horses over jumps and I simply cannot allow myself to think about danger. In fact the issue becomes so complicated, so twisted between fear and courage, between common sense and foolishness, that the more we try to analyse the risk of severe injury, the less clear it becomes. It is as though the mind has a valve which triggers a grey mist.

Ask any jockey about the possibility of a crippling injury and they will say: 'Yes, it could happen to me.' But deep down they don't acknowledge or believe it. The mind and body will not let us accept that possibility – it is a trait inherent in people in dangerous careers or who pursue high-risk activities. Other people are happy in a quieter life but for me the sharp edge of excitement, the pleasure of speed and a good horse, the need to make a living, all help to disperse the fear of injury. And if I sit quietly and think hard about the reality of a bad fall the valve switches on and the mist dulls the senses.

Rather than ponder the imponderable it is better to make a practical contribution on behalf of those who suffer long-term injuries. The Injured Jockeys Fund, which I contribute to, does tireless work for people who have been hurt while riding in races, and in addition I am always happy to get involved in raising funds for colleagues. I mentioned earlier in this book that I am passionate about golf, but playing in a fund-raising tournament for Shane in the year after his fall will always be one of the best rounds, regardless of the missed putts!

My own injuries to date have been relatively few and I count myself very fortunate. It makes me slightly nervous to say that as fate has a habit of altering things rapidly, but apart from a succession of collar-bone problems I cannot say injuries have hampered my career. The collar-bones were a problem when I was trying to get established – each time I seemed to get a run going I would have a fall and snap! This is a common injury for riders and is caused by putting your hand out to soften the fall – an instinctive reaction.

The more I broke my collar-bones (the right ten or 11 times, the left four times) the more brittle they became and it got to the stage where I was fit for two or three weeks then sidelined for a similar period of time, which was very frustrating. The left-hand bone has since been improved by an operation on the A/C (acromioclavicular) joint which had been pushed up by falls on my shoulder and the right-hand bone was effectively removed a couple of years ago. A third is all that is left and tissue forms there which, if I land on it, disintegrates and is sore for a day or two. This enables me to do two things – pull my shoulder round to point forward, a useless party trick which makes some people squeamish, and to walk away from falls which would once have KO'd me for at least two weeks. Taking this to a logical extreme, if they removed all my bones I could avoid injury completely, but what it would do for my posture doesn't bear thinking about! As it is, I have to force myself to sit up and back to avoid looking round-shouldered and after the operation I had to do a series of exercises to strengthen the area.

Other breaks include both ankles, the scaphoid bone (which sits at the base of the thumb), various hand bones and ribs, my wrist and coccyx (the tail-bone at the foot of my spine), while cuts and concussion have been commonplace over the years.

Each and every time a jockey falls from a horse they have to be examined by a doctor, either at the racecourse or a local GP, before they can ride again. This rule was brought in just a few years ago in a bid to prevent jockeys riding with broken bones, unwittingly or otherwise, or so completely dazed they had no recollection of events later. Doctors now have authority to prevent a jockey riding if they feel they are not fit, which can lead to squeals of discontent but in the main it makes sense to take medical advice.

Quite why some jump-jockeys go through a career avoiding serious injury, while others get so knocked about they eventually have to quit prematurely, is hard to say, although the combination of bone strength and ability to fall correctly are key factors. That does not explain why someone like Adrian Maguire can be seemingly indestructible for several seasons and then spend more time in hospital than Florence Nightingale. So tough was Adrian before his luck changed that we nicknamed him Rubber Man, a title conferred after a fall from a good horse called Capability Brown at Cheltenham. Riding in the Sun Alliance Chase won by Young Hustler, Adrian had an absolute bone-crusher of a fall and while he got to his feet he was so sore by the end of racing he had to be carried from the weighing-room. A visit to his doctor produced a remedy, however, and the following day he lifted Cool Ground to victory in the Gold Cup, producing an all-action finish in defiance of his condition 24 hours earlier.

Broken arms and numerous other injuries have plagued Adrian in recent seasons and his misery has been compounded by missing the Cheltenham Festival on at least a couple of occasions. At the other extreme is Richard Dunwoody, who at the end of the 1997–98 season had completed eight successive centuries, a measure of his ability to stay in one piece. In all that time I only remember him breaking his sternum, when See More Business fell in the 1997 Racing Post Chase, and on another occasion a bone in his hand. That's a remarkably trouble-free innings by a superb jockey whose ability to tuck up neatly when falling is a great virtue.

One fall of Richard's which I witnessed at close hand should be shown to every young rider as an example of what to do when a fall looms. On a horse called Dreamer's Delight in the Sun Alliance Novices' Hurdle, Richard was alongside another runner and vying for the lead as they headed for the second-last jump. Maximum speed was being produced, yet when Dreamer's Delight made a mistake Richard was in a roll before his horse fully hit the ground. He should have been knocked out for days yet was on his feet and walking away in less time than it takes to unbuckle a helmet.

The more falls you have the better you get at producing an injury-free technique but being in one piece after hitting the ground is one thing, avoiding the flailing hooves and legs of the horses is another. Many injuries happen this way, either as the jockey is falling through the air or lying on the turf. Getting into a good tuck and making yourself small and round so that the blows glance off your body is one survival hint, but it is a mighty relief to hear the last runner galloping through, particularly if you have fallen at the front of the pack and there are 20 horses behind you. Horses will not kick or tread on jockeys deliberately and the other riders are all trying to steer a course that takes them away from a prostrate colleague, but accidents happen.

Quite often in this sort of mêlée onlookers are wincing because the fallen horse has partly landed on its jockey.

Strangely enough that can be a good thing in that it creates a shield for the rider. The horse's frame, being bigger, is more easily spotted by the other runners and, while you don't want your horse to get to its feet and tread on you, while it lies still it is best to be grateful. Overhead a right din is going on, as horses clatter the hurdle top or brush the fence, jockeys shout and hooves pound – it is quite a way to earn a living. Once it has gone quiet you do a quick medical check, wiggle your arms and legs, then hopefully walk away with all parts still intact.

This has happened to me many times, but one occasion that sticks in my memory was slightly different. Riding a horse called Wheal Prosper at Newton Abbot on really heavy ground, we headed to the last fence in a three-mile novices' chase with the prize in the bag, all of 30 lengths clear of our nearest rival. It was not to be and as Wheal Prosper fell he rolled right over me.

Dazed, definitely confused and with bits of information telling my brain that we had been well clear, I reasoned that if I could find the darned horse there would be time to remount and still win, so I got to my feet. Wham! I was hit broadside by another runner, Tom Troubadour ridden by Hywel Davies, the force knocking both me and the horse over just as it was about to win. Hywel, who had a habit of calling everyone Matey, would usually ask a fallen jockey, 'Are you all right, Matey?' but on this occasion he kept repeating, 'What did you get up for, Matey? What did you get up for?' As luck would have it I was uninjured but it taught me not to stand up on the landing side of a fence. At about that time I also learnt not to hold on to the reins when unseating or falling from a horse. The result is bound to mean getting dragged, probably into the path of oncoming horses, who have no idea what you are going to do next, and it can result in a bad injury.

An alternative to getting dragged, is getting your foot hung up in the stirrup, which has happened to me once or twice, although thankfully I slipped free quite quickly. The notion of being really stuck turns my stomach over, and a film clip of an Australian race which I saw on television a few years ago fully conveyed what can happen: after a horse fell then regained its feet the poor jockey was dragged like a piece of cloth while his partner proceeded to jump several fences. He lived to tell the tale, but it looked awful.

Other accidents simply can never be predicted and when they happen all the skill in the world won't save a jockey from being placed in a perilous situation. One such incident happened to me in the autumn of 1998 and put me out of action for two weeks with a broken rib.

Riding a horse called Hippios at Plumpton, we galloped towards the first when he suddenly decided to refuse and slithered to a halt. Genuine horses with no ill-will refuse occasionally, particularly when tired at the end of a long race, but the field is usually well strung out by then and the refusing horse causes little or no obstruction. You should still check over your shoulder, however, before turning your horse to walk away in case another runner is coming up behind. When a refusal takes place early in a race the runners are usually still tightly packed. On Hippios I knew we were suddenly stuck like a broken-down vehicle in the fast lane of the motorway. Gritting my teeth, I prayed they would bypass us when I felt an almighty wallop in the back and found myself flying through the air. After a parabola which carried me five yards high and five yards wide, I landed in the grass, winded and gasping for breath. Apparently another runner had been unable to avoid us. In the horse's attempt to jump the hurdle, his head and chest had whacked me full in the back, shovelling me into space. There is an awful lot of power in half a ton of galloping thoroughbred. Jumping becomes instinctive for most horses when they are in a group – as the leaders jump the others prepare to do the same and, although I was in the way, the horse which had hit me was being told by its instincts, and training, to get airborne

Being on the injury list is no fun but I keep as fit as possible by doing exercises, not to develop muscle, which is three times heavier than fat, but to keep my blood circulating. Good blood circulation is one of the finest ways of speeding up the healing process and people often comment on how quickly I manage to return from injury, so it seems to work. With the rib injury I wanted to avoid jarring it, so I stopped riding horses until all pain had gone and instead did stretching exercises and used a mechanical walking machine at the local gym. Had I broken an ankle I would have been unable to use the walking machine but I would have used the rowing equivalent.

Another key factor in getting back to work is Rabbit Slattery, a physiotherapist based at Baydon near Swindon and daughter of Mary Bromiley, one of Britain's foremost equine chiropractors. Rabbit is not a qualified doctor but she is more beneficial to jockeys than the average GP because she has seen so many crocked riders and knows their individual injuries. In my case that means constant niggles in my lower back and neck, the result of a fall at Wincanton many years ago when my coccyx was cracked. Unfortunately, the back-protectors which we wear, and are in fact back-front-and-side protectors, add to this neck pain because they tend to hit the base of your neck when you fall.

Internal injuries, split livers and punctured lungs, are horrible and to be avoided, while head injuries are potentially the worst. For that reason the Jockey Club has tightened up on concussion injuries and ensure riders take time off accordingly. If a rider is dazed they have to take the rest of the day off; if they black-out for less than a minute they are on the sidelines for seven days; while more than a minute results in a 21-day lay-off. It is tough on riders who are knocked out briefly and then forced to miss rides in big races but it must make sense to anyone who believes there is a life after racing. Your brain takes a dreadful pounding if you get knocked out and the resulting bruising and swelling must be allowed time to disappear before you risk another blow.

That counts for little when a jockey is desperate to ride in a big race and there are times when a doctor says a jockey was out cold for a minute and 30 seconds while the patient claims it was less than a minute. In my experience racecourse doctors are not vindictive and will give a jockey the benefit of the doubt if there is only a few seconds involved.

Of course, it is not only for the jockey's benefit that riders are forced to take time off. A dazed or injured jockey cannot offer 100 per cent assistance to a horse, which is unfair on the owner, trainer, stable staff and punters. Yet there are times when jockeys ride with an injury, sometimes knowingly, sometimes in ignorance. This would be particularly true of young or struggling jockeys who dread being on the sidelines and missing opportunities and therefore they try to rush back from injury, something the Jockey Club attempts to eradicate by enforcing medical check-ups after falls. It is amazing how you can forget pain once the adrenaline gets going in a race, but we have all ridden with muscle aches and pains, or with discomfort from a bone fracture which has not healed properly. Any self-employed person would do the same and return to work early, although the older and wiser you get, the less tempted you are to rush back.

Unwittingly riding with a broken bone is not uncommon and stories of jockeys having falls then riding winners with fractured legs and arms add to the folklore concerning jump-racing's acts of heroism and madness. Perhaps the most common occurrence in this regard concerns rib injuries; getting winded in a fall is quite usual but it might be the following day before you realise the ache in your ribs is getting no better. An X-ray may reveal breaks or a sprung rib, in which the bone separates from the tissue on either side and moves out of line.

One thing is sure: as jockeys we are all extremely grateful to the medical teams which enable racing to take place. Our lives are in their hands on occasions and it is good to know they are not only competent but dedicated.

Coming back from injury is hard work, but at least it is not a daily battle, unlike dieting, which for me is the worst aspect of my job. If you have ever tried dieting you know it is hard work, requires dedication and an enormous amount of will power. It can be debilitating if you don't eat enough of the right food and a waste of time if you succumb to treats. Slavish devotion to dieting and the avoidance of certain culinary delights is part of the daily work regime for jockeys.

To make racing fair and competitive, horses have to carry mandatory weights, anything from 7st 7lb to 10st-plus on the flat and from 10st to 12st-plus over jumps in Britain, while in Ireland the minimum weight over jumps is 9st 7lb. Occasionally, all the horses in a race carry the same weight, but normally there are differences caused by issues such as weight allowances for fillies or mares and weight penalties for past winners. More extreme differences occur in handicaps, when the best horse may be 'handicapped' with 35lb or more than their worst rival.

No horse can run in a race until its jockey, complete with saddle and all the paraphernalia, has been weighed at the course by an official – known as the clerk of the scales – to ensure the correct weight is carried. Trainers book jockeys in the belief their animal won't be burdened with unnecessary extra weight, which is where dieting comes in since most jockeys cannot make the lighter weights naturally. There are a few lucky ones who eat what they want, especially while young.

Whether a pound or two of weight makes any difference to half a ton of fit thoroughbred is a moot point, but if a horse is beaten the minimum distance of a short head there will be people who say it does. As a jockey you simply cannot put yourself in that position and it is better to be honest with a trainer or owner and say in advance if you think you will struggle to do the weight. If they then book you and you make the weight, that is fine.

Sadly for me weight is a serious problem, although advances in diet research has made life considerably easier. Gone are the days when a jockey had to eat very small portions of food, the secret now being to eat plenty of food which your body readily digests and avoid things which it cannot break down. These diets are not cheap but the one I am currently using, supplied by a company called NuTron Laboratories, seems to be working satisfactorily. Initially it involved giving them a blood sample which, after analysis, showed which foods my body digests and those it does not. I can now eat as much beef and potatoes as I like, but I have to avoid cheese and mushrooms. Cod is okay, crab is not, coffee and alcohol are out, tea and fruit juice are in. Jane is very supportive in my battle to stick to this diet, but she dislikes it because it is rather bland and gives her little scope to experiment when cooking.

In company with Andrew Thornton this dieting affliction hits me as hard as anyone in the weighing-room and by God have I suffered on occasions. Yet it is not simply about food intake; increasingly it is a science of the mind as well as the body and while there was a time when I would merely give up eating for a few days to lose a few pounds that is now no longer feasible.

I am no longer a teenager and the combination of my age (28), my build and a very busy schedule means I need a clear and focused mind as well as muscular strength and stamina. After ten years of weight-watching it is more important than ever that I don't become morose about dieting and also that its place in my life is managed. I owe that both to myself and Jane.

The height of a person often has little bearing on their weight – a six-foot-tall person of slim build can be lighter than the chunky chap eight inches smaller. In my case I am not only quite tall at 5ft 10in but I am solidly built and the mental and physical strain I put upon myself to ride at 10st 2lb, which is now the lightest I manage, takes its toll.

At the end of the 1997–98 season, the first in which I rode 100 winners, I was absolutely exhausted by this routine and desperately in need of a holiday. I rode six winners in June 1998, the start of the new season, a good base from which to begin the campaign for anyone pursuing the jockeys' championship, but I was dead on my feet and simply going through the motions before Jane and I took a fortnight's holiday abroad.

Two days before we were due to leave, I was offered a ride in a chase by trainer Andy Hobbs on a horse called Moorland Highflyer. He seemed to have a very good chance of winning, but I knew that a fall could jeopardise the holiday, and it would be very damaging mentally not to get away and break the regime. While I pondered the offer of the ride I realised there was no way I should take it. By merely questioning whether it was the right thing to do I was emphatically stating it was the wrong thing – you simply cannot point a horse at a line of fences unless you are totally committed, otherwise it is dangerous. I turned the ride down and Moorland Highflyer won, but I had no regrets. Mentally, I was in no state to carry on and, while I am not saying that the rides I did take before the holiday made me a liability to other jockeys (and before the Jockey Club medical adviser pays me a visit), what I am saying is that experience had shown I could go so far but no further. The scales cannot lie and I knew it was time for a break: my resolve had weakened and my weight was shooting up – having been down to 10st 2lb in February I was up to 11st just prior to the holiday. This had one benefit because I wanted to be very choosy about which horses I rode in that time and, since better-class horses carry bigger weights in handicaps, I was still able to fulfil my obligations.

Later, during the holiday and while lying on the beach, another 5lb was added, but a few games of golf and a bit of running began to trim the figure and by the time I was ready to ride again in late July I was down to 10st 10lb and feeling very fit and refreshed and ready, mentally, to tackle the annual weight-reduction slog. It takes a long time to get my weight down towards its minimum but it is not too difficult keeping there when the season gets busy. A steady routine helps, but in January 1999 the weather made life very difficult for me. I was to ride a hotly fancied horse called Get Real who was to carry just 10st 1lb in the Victor Chandler Chase at Ascot, one of the season's feature races for two-mile chasers. By sitting in the sauna on the eve of the race I managed to get down to 10st 2lb but the meeting was abandoned because of waterlogging. The race was then carried over to the following Friday's card at the same track and I went through the same preparation, with the added pressure that this was a big race and I had to be as close as I could to the horse's allotted handicap weight – the press were bound to comment if my excess weight was deemed to have cost us the race.

To my utter dismay the rearranged race also hit by the weather and it was delayed for a further 24 hours and would be held at Kempton. This was prolonging my discomfort and calling upon yet another visit to the sauna. When racing finally took place, I was faced with eight races while at my lightest and although I managed to lose another pound – and therefore did not put up overweight – it was a tough time, not helped when we were beaten by a head into second place. Adrenaline kept me going throughout the afternoon and I had the consolation of riding three winners, but the effort took its toll and I was utterly exhausted after racing. It took me most of the next day to recover.

I have tried many different kinds of diets offered by friends and professionals who say their methods of weight loss are the best. I well remember the 'cookie diet', recommended by former jockey Jamie Railton, which involved eating a cookie and drinking a glass of water three times a day and allowing yourself one meal in the evening. It worked quite well for a while but was very boring and once I lost interest it was time to try something else.

Various pills have been offered to me and one that worked successfully had plenty of goodness, minerals and proteins, but was expensive and there are only so many times you can sit down to a nourishing meal of a pill.

Not surprisingly, jockeys have been known to go to pretty desperate lengths to lose weight. A rumour went around a couple of years ago that some flat jockeys were bulimic – eating and then making themselves sick. It is not something I have tried but not all my attempts at weight loss have been healthy.

Dehydration through sweating is not recommended by your average GP and while many people spend leisure time in saunas, it is little fun putting on a rubber sweat-suit and turning up the car heater to maximum before undertaking a lengthy drive to the races, something I have done many times. You get unbearably hot, the sweat pours from the pores and I have lost three or four pounds from an already-starved body on occasions. This method sometimes needs a little encouragement to start working and there have been times when I have been forced to stop the car and run up and down the road to get the metabolism heated up before I continue on the journey.

How I wished I had worn my sweat-suit in the car on my first visit to Aintree. I had gone there to ride a horse called Skinnhill for Tim Thompson Jones in the John Hughes Chase, two days before the Grand National and, having arrived in good time, went out to familiarise myself with the course and its legendary fences. It was a thrill to be there and I felt rather good about life as I took a leisurely stroll into the changing-room where I intended to continue taking things easy by putting my feet up in the sauna and shedding a couple of pounds.

The casual demeanour ended and panic-stricken horror swept over me when I asked directions to the sweat room. 'There isn't one,' came the reply. I was truly stunned that one of Britain's foremost tracks had no sauna, although one has since been installed.

I knew it would not look good for a young jockey to put up overweight in an important race but I was not alone – Peter

Niven had arrived a couple of pounds heavier than he intended and also needed to lose weight. We got around the problem by making our own sauna: I piled on as many clothes as I could find and borrowed Peter Scudamore's track suit and sweat jacket. We then ran on the spot for 40 minutes in the drying room with two large tumble-driers turned fully up and churning round with their doors open. We came out looking like two stuffed and basted turkeys, but I had managed to shed 3lb.

Sweating has its uses and I still resort to it when necessary but it is not permanent weight loss and you soon put it back on when you take in fluid. The yo-yo effect of sweating and then drinking, sweating and drinking, is obviously not good for the body.

Laxatives make me sick when I think about them now, but I tried them when I was in my late teens. As I was still struggling to become established as a jockey I often didn't know where or when I would next be asked to ride in a race, so there was no continuity about the job or the diet. Taking laxatives could make a difference in a short space of time, and since I was trying to ride at about 9st 12lb they seemed a good option.

Ugh, what a horrible business. When the instructions on the box said take two, I would take four in a desperate bid to shed a few extra ounces. The time and place you took them was crucial if you weren't to be caught short and out of reach of a toilet – the prospect of going nightclubbing and finding a queue for the loo was too dreadful a possibility to contemplate. Friends had said it was potentially risky to take them before sleeping for fear that you wouldn't wake up, but believe me, you do. The warning began in the stomach, which would groan and churn like a cauldron, and it was then prudent to get up and head for the bathroom at a good pace. Farting was particularly dangerous.

I have few fond memories of laxatives but they were handy when we needed to teach another lad a lesson while I was working in Hertfordshire for trainer John Jenkins – my first job in Britain after I left Ireland. Money was tight, so it was not amusing when food kept disappearing from the cupboard and while we knew who the culprit was, it was hard to deter him. Someone suggested laxatives in chocolate form and after buying a bar and making it look as though it had been half eaten, the remainder was placed in the fridge. Sure enough, the bait was taken and we were doubled up with silent laughter the following morning when a very ashen-looking lad came down the yard with a string of toilet paper hanging out of his pocket. At lunch-time he sat quietly at the table unwilling to eat, his eyes sunken to the back of his head.

What must be borne in mind is that the overweight jockey is not only going to reduce his horse's chances of winning, he is also going to annoy the trainer and owner and gain a reputation for being unable to do specified weights. Desperate men use desperate measures to avoid this tag and while security is tight and there is virtually no chance of cheating these days, tales from the racecourse include the trick of sitting on the scales wearing paper-thin boots with no soles before returning to the changing-room to put on proper leather boots for the race. After the race, if in the first four, the same jockey would have to weigh in and while unable to put on the paper boots would get away with being a little heavier since this is allowed for clothing and tack getting wet.

A variation on that theme was provided by a jockey who retired not long ago who used to put a piece of coat hanger wire down his breeches and boots so that a bit of the wire protruded through a hole in the sole. By sitting on the scale, with his foot hovering just above the floor, he could gently push against the wire and weigh out at the correct weight. Other dodges included weighing out with the number cloth draped over a saddle which had the stirrups and leathers removed, or getting on the scales having removed the obligatory back-protector, but these and other ways of getting around the rules are not something I would recommend. Getting caught would mean a fine and suspension and doubtless a lot of very damaging publicity – owners would lose trust and, besides, if you are riding six times in an afternoon you don't want to be messing about with bits of equipment. Rather than cheat, put pressure on myself and reduce the horse's chance of winning, I trust a sensible diet and lightweight riding gear.

The diet I used during 1997–98 was a big help during my successful bid to ride 100 winners in a season. Inevitably, I was forced to do a lot of travelling to meetings and did not want the additional hassle and wasted hours spent sitting in saunas sweating the weight off – dehydrating yourself in that way is more debilitating than any other method, although it is extremely useful when you need to shed a pound or two in a hurry.

Until I allowed science to dictate my sensible diet I had to spend at least one or two sessions in the sauna each day, no fun if it meant coming home from the races at seven or eight in the evening, having a light meal and then sitting in the sweat-box for an hour. It certainly felt like a waste of time and is not fair on a wife who might like to talk to her husband. With the new diet my weight is under control and I spend time when I come home from the races with Jane. In the morning the same benefits occur, so, after riding out I can return home and read the papers before going racing, rather than sit among the steam upstairs.

All jockeys are offered diets and we pass the information around, although they are only as good as the person's will power to stick rigidly to them. The lure of riding good horses and winning big races is as much incentive as I need.

On the face of it, my current food intake appears quite tasty and offers a fair bit of variety, but remember, snacks involving even one chocolate, a biscuit or piece of cheese are forbidden. Disciplining yourself to say no is not easy, particularly when you feel tired and hungry and the petrol station where you have stopped for fuel is offering shelves of snacks.

Until I tried this diet I did not eat anything before midday. Before that, and because I like eating chocolate, I would treat myself to a Twirl on the way to the races – that would be my breakfast and lunch and I really looked forward to undoing the wrapper and enjoying the hedonism of the first scrummy mouthful. In itself, the Twirl was not going to put pounds on, but dieting is about balance and the breakfast I eat now complements the food I eat the rest of the week – and there is no place for chocolate. Everything in this diet has to be additive-free and pure natural goodness. The success has shown that controlled eating – that is correct quantities of the right food at set times – is better than a random routine.

One drawback of the NuTron diet is that it bars me from

drinking alcohol and while in recent years I only allowed myself two or three glasses of wine on Saturday nights when we went out with friends, that is now a past pleasure. A pity, since Sunday is generally a day off but no less important for that. Being wound up about the work–diet regime is not good, so Sunday is a day to unwind – Jane and I get up reasonably late, take the dog for a walk and veg out in front of the TV, relaxing in readiness for the coming week.

Whether I'm relaxing or having a hard day at the office I smoke cigarettes, about 30 a day usually, a habit started when I was a teenager and smoking meant being part of the crowd. The fact that many jockeys smoke may come as a shock to people who assume sportsmen and women are fitness freaks who avoid the weed, but apart from the fact that I have smoked all my adult life, I regard cigarettes as part of my weight-loss regime. Although I know of no scientific link between smoking and weight, I find picking up a cigarette is an alternative to putting food in my mouth – Adrian Maguire's weight went up 10lb when he temporarily gave up, although that might not happen in every person's case. Smoking is merely my personal preference. I acknowledge that in tests non-smokers have the edge in fitness, but I believe I work harder to achieve fitness because I smoke. I enjoy smoking so I use that as a piece of psychology which gives me an incentive. If I felt I was not as fit as another jockey it would be time to give up, and with so many good young lads coming through you have to be committed 100 per cent to maintain your position.

On the issue of fitness the only way to achieve maximum strength and stamina for riding in races is to do just that: ride. There is no way you can get there by running, cycling, swimming or any other healthy pursuit. The more you ride in races the fitter you get, the more you push and shove horses from the saddle the longer you can do it for. Tony McCoy and Richard Johnson are two of the fittest jockeys I know, and it is no coincidence that they also ride in the most races.

Starving, sweating, suffering injuries and getting beaten when you expect to win, are the worst aspects of the job, but the endless hours on the road travelling to meetings are not much fun either.

Yearly mileage for busy jockeys will involve between 50,000 and 60,000 miles by road, plus flights to meetings in Ireland and occasionally further afield. Not all those miles are done in one car, and living in Oxfordshire means there are plenty of jockeys near by with whom I share lifts: Johnny Kavanagh, Rodney Farrant, Timmy Murphy, Glenn Tormey, Jim Culloty, Adrian Maguire, Brendan Powell and Carl Llewellyn to name a few. That said I have been averaging 3,800 miles a month in my own car, about 45,000 miles a year, which is tough on the vehicle, a 2.5 litre V6 Mondeo, and not much fun for the driver. That average does not reveal the whole story, since it includes quieter summer months when we might only travel to two or three meetings a week, or time spent on the sidelines through injury or suspension; in busy months the average mileage shoots up.

I've only missed one ride through arriving late at a meeting, and it was not a nice experience, fretting and sweating at the wheel while stuck in traffic. It happened when I tried to ride at two meetings in one day and, having done the job at Newbury, set off for Ludlow but got snarled up in a roadworks jam near Cirencester in Gloucestershire. Eventually getting on to the open road I put my foot down, arrived at the course and ran to the weighing-room knowing I had to be on and off the scales at least 15 minutes before the race – I missed the deadline by 30 seconds but escaped a fine by the stewards because of the roadworks. Such mishaps have been mercifully rare for me, but jockeys do miss rides when traffic grinds to a halt and the stewards hand out fines, particularly when they feel that by trying to ride at two meetings a jockey has not allowed enough time to get to the second venue. No excuses can be entertained since the stewards know what time the jockey left the previous meeting by noting the time of the race in which he last took part. My own rule of thumb is to assess the time it will take to get to a meeting by making a note of advertised delays or the added congestion normal at big fixtures, then add one and a half hours. That normally takes care of traffic jams, punctured tyres and so on, but I also try to narrow down the likelihood of problems en route by driving decent cars, well serviced and preferably low mileage. A sponsored car helps and if it has a bit of acceleration even better! Many racecourses are placed in rural locations and involve driving on single carriageways, so it helps if you can get past slow-moving vehicles.

In all businesses there are occasions when the question has to be asked: 'Is this journey the right thing to do?' But the answer for a jockey always has to be 'yes'. Our reasons for doing so are not entirely altruistic, for although it is always an added pleasure to ride horses for old friends and acquaintances, the reason we set off for rides in far-off places is because it could lead to more work in the future. It is not as though you can phone the customer (the owner or trainer) and say, 'I'm coming up that way at the end of the month, is it okay if I ride the horse then?' The race meeting will be long gone.

Yet that situation confronts jockeys regularly as they consider round-trips totalling hundreds of miles for maybe one or two rides on horses which have little chance of winning. It is a grim prospect on occasions, and both flat and jump-jockeys face particular difficulties, the former because the roads are busiest in summer, the latter because much of their driving is done in poor weather and darkness.

For me that part of the job has become slightly easier as I have established myself and I no longer feel so bad if I turn the odd ride down. It is not easy, particularly as it took me a long time to get going and in those early days it was unthinkable to reject a ride, no matter how far the journey or useless the horse.

Now all my rides are handled by my agent and while on most occasions he can confirm a booking as soon as someone phones him, he does check with his jockeys before committing them to a very long journey for one ride.

The bottom line is that you only get out of the job what you put into it.

VI

Jockeys and the Weighing-room

An afternoon at the races can be quite an adventure for a jump-jockey so I don't look for any added excitement on the way. Avoiding, whenever possible, one of those tortuous dashes through traffic, I arrive in good time and head for the weighing-room. Tennis players prepare in the locker-room, footballers disappear into the tunnel, golfers go to the changing-room and jockeys assemble in the weighing-room, a bit of a misnomer since it is not the place where we are officially weighed – that takes place in a room known as 'the scales', where the weight each horse is allotted to carry is checked by the clerk of the scales.

The weighing which does take place in the weighing-room involves a trial run before we go through to the scales, but the weighing-room's importance is significant. It is a haven for jockeys and their valets, a secluded place, away from perhaps tens of thousands of racegoers, a place where we meet, swap gossip, change into our colours, boots and breeches and mentally prepare for the challenges ahead. Apart from officials of the racecourse no one else can enter, which gives us the chance to get ready without distractions and also keeps security tight. The idea that someone might want to bribe a jockey just before a race might seem far-fetched, but if a big enough bet has been placed the temptation to try might get to a gambler. In addition, the chances of anyone tampering with our kit, including the all-important saddle, are unlikely because of this ban on outsiders.

The weighing-room is my first port of call when I arrive at the races. There I liaise with my valet, eat my lunch, read the paper and get changed ready for my first ride of the day, stopping to chat to my colleagues or slipping out to speak to trainers while passing the time. Jockeys choose to prepare mentally in different ways but I have no hard and fast pre-race preparation, except that I simply don't like to put myself under too much pressure.

Chat among jockeys is no different from that in any workplace but tactics are discussed before a race, generally fairly briefly, and relate usually to who might make the running, who is on a horse that wants to be held up and any idiosyncrasies which the runners might possess. If a horse has a tendency to jump left or right or run down its fences, meaning it swerves three or four strides from the fence, a jockey might pass this information on, not because they want to jeopardise their chances of winning but to reduce the risk of anyone getting hurt. Sometimes you have to be a bit coy about your horse's chances but it is generally better to be honest if asked a straight question. It is not in your interest to tell your colleagues you plan to make the running only to ride a waiting race near the back of the field. You don't want to make enemies in that way and since the spirit in the jump-jockeys' weighing-room is so positive and invariably friendly and there is a great feeling of camaraderie, there is no point in spoiling that by acting out of character.

We are all members of the Jockeys Association of Great Britain (JAGB) and often turn to that organisation and its secretary, Michael Caulfield, when we are faced with a work-related problem. It must be one of the few organisations with 100 per cent membership. Since Michael joined the Association ten years ago he has never had to ask a jockey to join, we all did so voluntarily with the effect that some 500 riders are on the books. Of those, about 350 are conditional or apprentice jockeys.

When you think of great jockeys of the past, men like Sir Gordon Richards and Fred Archer on the flat, Fred Winter and Tim Molony over jumps, it is hard to believe they had no representation and, until the formation of the JAGB in 1969, they had neither a right to appeal against a decision on the racecourse nor to payment at source; they simply invoiced owners and waited for a cheque. The JAGB has organised pensions, insurance and job-training schemes for all members, and altered the way jockeys are regarded by other groups within racing. If we feel a suspension or fine unfair or if we are

Rough Quest carries me across the line at Aintree to win the
1996 Grand National (*Daily Star*)

Rough Quest gives me a kiss during a photo-call for the press the day after our National win; trainer Terry Casey is on the right
(*Daily Star*)

Me and Jane 24 hours after the Grand National win. We got married a few months later (*Daily Star*)

The schooling grounds at Seven Barrows. The mix of hurdles and fences are some of the best in Britain (*John Beasley*)

Riding Ardentinny at Seven Barrows. Strangely enough, Ardentinny is the only grey among 100 horses trained by Nicky Henderson in the 1998–99 season (*John Beasley*)

It's better to make mistakes at home than at the races. Royal Toast has made a hash of this fence and broken the wooden rail, and the deceleration has lifted me from the saddle (*John Beasley*)

Johnny Kavanagh is riding in front of me on Garrison Friendly (*John Beasley*)

The Governor and I ponder a mass of options in the office
at Seven Barrows (*John Beasley*)

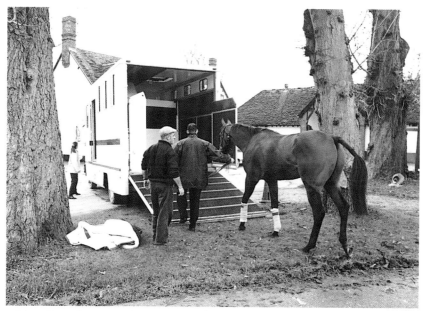

It's off to the races for a runner from Seven Barrows (*John Beasley*)

Johnny Worrall has worked for the Governor since 1978 and is one of the long-serving staff members vital to a big yard (*John Beasley*)

ABOVE AND OPPOSITE: different silks, different races, same result, as I ride Katarino and Stormyfairweather to victory at Cheltenham
(*John Beasley*)

Riding a winner at Cheltenham is a great feeling. I am on the left
with Stormyfairweather on our way to winning the Novices' Chase.
Skycab and Philip Hide are keeping us company
(*John Beasley*)

OPPOSITE PAGE TOP: in the winners' enclosure at Cheltenham I give an
account of the race to the Governor while his wife Diana (*left*) looks
on (*John Beasley*)
BOTTOM: riding Remittance Man (*second on left*) in the Queen
Mother Champion Chase, Cheltenham, 1994 (*John Beasley*)

In reflective mood while wearing the Queen Mother's colours

summoned to the Jockey Club to answer a charge of breaking the rules we get the backing of a solicitor paid for by the JAGB. At £1,200 a day that is a cost which most jockeys simply could not afford.

In short, the jockeys now have teeth, and while the great riders of the past were apparently revered for their skill and heroic deeds, their work was based on a master–servant relationship with owners and, to a lesser degree, trainers. Michael Caulfield and the JAGB have been battling to end this attitude which, he says, has been the biggest stumbling block in the battle to acquire sponsorship for jockeys. The argument that clashes could occur between a jockey and owner's sponsor was only part of the problem, says Michael, who believes jealousy by a small minority of owners in authority caused delays in getting approval for sponsorship. The image of jockeys as forelock-tugging little men apparently lives on in the minds of a few, and while I keep my head down and work hard to do a job, it is good to know the JAGB is doing its best to secure rights which other sportsmen and women enjoy. Michael looks out for us because our careers are ending before many people have thought of starting a family.

Richard Dunwoody OBE is the unofficial senior jockey and he serves on a JAGB panel which discusses issues relating to the profession. This seniority does not mean we give him any advantage in a race or treat him differently out of the saddle. He gained this position when Peter Scudamore retired, an act which led to a time-honoured tradition: we all turned up for work the next day and moved our clothes up one peg.

This does not mean there is a regimented line of importance around the room – the need to be near your valet means that all the jockeys looked after by the same valet stick together, and because I am heavy and through an afternoon regularly switch from normal riding apparel into lightweight kit, my valet, John Buckingham, likes me to sit in the corner. He says I make the place untidy otherwise.

Scu is irreplaceable as an ambassador for jockeys – he and Declan Murphy were not only top riders but also very appro-achable and young jockeys were always asking their advice. Richard does a good job representing us as a group, and he is helped in that role by Brendan Powell who is number two. Some way down the list is Tony McCoy, twice champion jockey but still relatively junior in a situation where age and experience are more important. My own position, on the southern and Midlands' circuit, is among a group consisting of Chris Maude, Carl Llewellyn and Paul Holley – if this were a boardroom with Richard as chairman and Brendan his deputy, we would be among the committee members.

Richard is the ultimate professional and with two Grand National wins to his name is as well known outside of racing as any jump-jockey. That fame, his consummate talent in the saddle, his experience over many years and his OBE all make him an excellent member of the Jockeys Association panel. When it comes to negotiating on our behalf, Richard has the credentials which give him authority, whether he is talking to the senior steward of the Jockey Club, the chairman of the British Horseracing Board or the marketing director of a blue-chip company.

He is also very single-minded, and while he gets fully involved in working with the JAGB to better conditions for his colleagues, he is adept, some would say ruthless, at looking after himself. If a jockey takes a fall and looks unlikely to ride again that day much furtive rustling of the racecard takes place as colleagues assess whether the injured person's absence means a decent horse is without a rider. We don't want to be seen to be dancing on the poor bloke's grave but business is business and we all accept that position. Yet Richard is the master at doing this research almost before the person has hit the floor. If you go to find the trainer of the spare horse you can bet he got there first. I call that professionalism and while there are times when nobody else matters but Woody, that is probably the best way to be.

Away from the racecourse Richard is good company, entertaining and charming, but in the weighing-room he is a loner, a deep thinker who prefers his own company, a meticulous planner of tactics and observer of horses. This concentration suits him. Other riders do it differently but we are all preparing for action and what could be our finest ride, our funniest, the most notorious, the most painful, yes, and even our last. It could also be an epoch which leads to a string of big-race winners. In that atmosphere some jockeys chat, some are quiet, some make jokes, some are busy, some contemplative. Naturally there is added excitement and tension at big meetings.

There has been no finer jump-jockey than Richard. He is the ultimate talent, strong, stylish and a man who builds an intangible bond with racehorses. While Tony McCoy has smashed all sorts of records in the past couple of seasons – fastest 50, fastest 100, fastest 200, most winners in a season, etc. – he still has some way to go to be as good as Richard, particularly in his use of the whip, a wonderful tool of the trade when used effectively, an ugly cudgel when misused. No one pulls it through from one side of the horse to the other with more finesse than Richard, and few can match him in using it with equal dexterity in left and right hand. He was one of the first riders to perfect this ambidexterity and since he was the man to emulate, young riders made big efforts to practise using the whip in both hands. For me this was relatively easy, since I was born left-handed but was forced to become right-handed by the nuns at my first convent school. I now write, think and play golf right-handed but have retained equality in my left hand.

A phenomenon called Tony McCoy has hit racing, but I don't think he is a better rider than me. You could argue that Tony rode 253 winners in 1997–98 while I achieved a personal best of 102, but our circumstances are different. Can anyone be sure that Kieren Fallon is a better rider than Frankie Dettori just because he is the champion jockey? Besides, jockeys cannot allow themselves to think they are inferior to another rider; there is no place for negativity in this business and since we all start at the same point in a race, we are all equal. Racegoers and fans of racing will debate jockeys' talents, but they can only be subjective.

Tony, known in the weighing-room as AP after his initials, is a great advertisement for racing, very level-headed and a nice fellow who respects senior colleagues and is happy to give advice to other youngsters. He would do anything for you and he sets an example when appearing in public, which should be a rule of thumb for every aspiring jockey. As a person I wouldn't fault him, but neither would I always give him top marks for the way he uses his whip. Use of the whip has been a very touchy subject for years and AP has come under more scrutiny for the strength and style with which he administers it than any other jump-jockey and he has paid the penalty by being suspended on many occasions. I know he is attempting to alter this while still squeezing out every possible winning opportunity and he is experimenting with air-cushioned whips which are less severe, but if he doesn't find an acceptable formula he will suffer further suspensions. By the time this book is published he might have settled on a new style; I hope so because so many youngsters want to emulate him.

He is very stylish when riding a finish and television cameras give some wonderful close-ups of him in action, but the whip rules mean there is constant monitoring of force and frequency and they are the facets which AP must address. It might cost him a race or two but that is better than a suspension – and if other jockeys are prepared to knuckle down and fulfil the disciplines of the whip rule, so must he or the whole thing becomes a joke.

It is to AP's credit that he has taken the opportunities that have come his way and capitalised on them in emphatic style, setting numerous records in a very short time. As a champion jockey he has achieved something to which most of his colleagues aspire. I would love to be champion jockey and it was long an ambition of mine but I now accept the championship is unlikely to come my way. That is not being negative but it is being a realist. To win the title you need to be totally focused on riding winners 12 months of the year, a gruelling task now that racing takes place through the summer and means would-be champions can barely take a day off. I suspect future champions will be younger than in the past for that reason.

AP comes into that category and it has helped that he is associated with the sport's most successful trainer, Martin Pipe, a man whose pursuit of winners involves training a huge string of horses and actively pursuing races of any description, from lowly selling races in midsummer to the big prizes at the spring festivals.

I am very happy to ride for the stables I do because I know there are some very good horses there, but I simply don't have the firepower, the quantity of horses, at my disposal to become champion. In addition, the battle with my weight means I focus first and foremost on doing my very best for the stables I ride for. That drives me on, not the thought of chasing a title, although I would give it my best shot if circumstances changed radically.

The whole issue of realism is extremely tricky for jump-jockeys. On the one hand we have to believe that anything is possible, otherwise we would be turning down rides on every horse which doesn't start favourite; on the other hand, if you question what you are doing you are being defeatist, a damning state of mind and wholly unforgiving in such a dangerous job. If you are not totally committed when you sit on a horse at the start of a race you increase your chances of defeat at best and injury at worst.

Brendan Powell has been around a long, long time but no one doubts that at 38 he is riding as well as ever. He too has a Grand National to his name, having won it in 1988 on Rhyme 'n' Reason, and he, above all jockeys, lives for racing. While the rest of us enjoy a day off and time away from horses, Brendan cannot wait to get back in the saddle. If the only meeting of the day is at Perth in Scotland and Brendan gets the chance of one ride he goes there, despite the fact that he lives in Oxfordshire!

Perhaps because of the element of risk, jump-jockeys are very loath to brag. If a jockey manages to secure a contract with a yard or picks up a decent spare ride in a big race they are likely to keep quiet, as though counting their chickens would be tempting disaster. Besides, people read the racing press and know soon enough when a jockey has achieved a breakthrough so we tend not to make a big thing of it among our colleagues.

On the other hand, if I hear that a friend in the weighing-room has been given a winning chance I am only too happy to say 'well done' and wish them the best of luck. I remember how important those little breaks were when I was getting started and a pat on the back helped my confidence. Simon McNeill, who retired very recently at the age of 42, was perhaps the first senior jockey to notice me and wish me luck when I was getting going and I'll always be grateful to him for that.

The 'Mr Steady' of the weighing-room is Carl Llewellyn, whose dual Grand National wins on Party Politics and Earth

Summit have been the highlights in a career which once threatened to be wrecked by injury. What with breaking his leg twice and suffering from an attack of Hepatitis B, Carl suffered badly in the past and it often stopped him just when he was making an ascent in the pecking order. He missed out on several big winners during those times but he is quietly determined and reliable, the sort to get back almost unnoticed. He has the respect of his colleagues for that.

Norman Williamson is another top-flight rider, and with Dave Roberts booking his rides he is always a participant in the big races. He will be able to dine out until he dies on his memorable Cheltenham Festival of 1995 when four winners included the Gold Cup and Champion Hurdle double on Master Oats and Alderbrook. While many of the top jockeys riding in Britain were born in Ireland – a country where horses are part of the furniture and a big percentage of people own or have an involvement with one – most settle away from home and return only to ride at selected meetings. Norman has always managed to maintain a big involvement with Irish racing and rides there regularly while still keeping British trainers happy with his availability. Many of his big winners have been supplied by Kim Bailey and while the relationship ended briefly, after a liaison between Norman and Kim's now-estranged wife Tracey which gave the Sunday tabloids some juicy material, that matter has been forgotten. It says much about Kim that he was big enough to accept it was in the past and to recognise that Norman was a good man to have in the saddle. Norman has recently found a rich seam of winners through his association with Herefordshire trainer Venetia Williams. The victories of Teeton Mill, Venetia's best horse to date, have shown Norman as an ice-cool rider on the big occasion.

I will always have an empathy with Andy Thornton because, like me, he struggles hard to beat the scales and his success, gained the hard way by clawing up the ranks, is a lesson in never giving up. True, some doors opened for him on the way, and his spare-ride success on See More Business in the King George VI Chase at Kempton on Boxing Day 1997 is an illustration of that, but Andy has capitalised on those opportunities because he has talent and you have to respect that. His

King George win and the subsequent victory on Cool Dawn in the Gold Cup were reward for years of slogging up and down motorways and riding horses of any type. A former champion amateur, Andy was exceptionally 'boggy' when he started, jockeys' slang for not very polished, and while he is as neat as he can be today, his style remains unique. He is a big lad and it took him quite some time to ascertain how long to set his stirrup leathers – too long and you look like a huntsman, too short and you are unsteady.

Andy now rides longer than anyone, but he has a very good seat on a horse – he is as one with his partner and very difficult to shed – and, most importantly, horses run for him. While the rest of us are effectively riding above our horses, Andy is almost sitting in the saddle.

Chris Maude's career has run parallel to mine, although it seemed that when he was up I was down and vice versa. We worked our way through from being conditional jockeys and became established as senior pros and while we both have ambitions to attain we are associated with yards which offer us the chance of fulfilment – Chris is effectively number two to AP at Martin Pipe's and he should get plenty more winners while that arrangement lasts.

Adrian Maguire, first jockey to the powerful David Nicholson stable and a dynamo until injuries began hitting him, and Richard Johnson, his deputy at that yard and a young man in a hurry, terrifically fit and strong and with no weight worries, are both likely to be champion jockeys. Northern-based riders Tony Dobbin and Peter Niven are less likely to achieve that title, since there are fewer meetings in their area, but few would deny they are masters of their trade. All these lads will look back on their careers with a sense of achievement, but each day I see jockeys who I feel frustrated for because they are so under-rated. Top of my list has to be Gerry Hogan.

I have seen some wonderful jockeys in the years I have been riding, and I have witnessed several from the day they started – AP and Adrian Maguire spring to mind. Basing my view on the talents I have seen in all these good riders it must be one of the greatest travesties of modern racing that Gerry has not made it as one of the top jockeys – and I can honestly say that has nothing to do with the fact that I know him and count him as a friend. No doubt sportsmen and women the world over can identify people in their sport whose talent aches to be released on to the big stage and on a regular basis.

Gerry is simply a great rider. He has a beautiful pair of hands – meaning he has a natural talent for pacifying horses and getting them to do what he wants – and has the situation under control long before a fight occurs. When I look at Gerry on a horse I want to stop the action; he has the definitive seat for a jockey and it is a quality which should be studied by anyone interested in racing. Despite the fact he is 6ft he is very neat and stylish and there is no hustle and bustle when he rides, an inborn quality which cannot be manufactured. This enables young horses to come out of a race having learnt something without being totally physically exhausted and thinking to themselves, 'What on earth have I been through?'

Others don't have Gerry's talents and seem to have little chance of making it through the ranks, but I don't begrudge them for trying and, besides, they are getting paid at the same rate as the champion jockey. They love the thrill of riding winners, something which long-retired jockeys still admit takes some beating, and as long as they don't get in my way in a race, that's fine. There are two or three who should not be riding, who are so inept as to be an embarrassment to the trade; they look out of control when asked to ride difficult horses and you also come across the occasional amateur who fits that category. I would add, though, that the standard of riding in races among the unpaid ranks is generally very high.

A change in the rules in 1998 means that stable staff can now take part in races as amateurs, and since many were doing so anyway and getting round the old rule by calling themselves pupil assistant trainers it needed updating. The standard of amateur riders can only go up if they start off working in yards, maybe only for a season or two, learn the ropes, ride out three or four horses each day and generally get fitter and more competent in the saddle.

The weighing-room would be hard-pressed to function without valets. A quaint but rather dated term, a valet, according to Chambers Dictionary, is 'a manservant who attends to clothes and toilet'. Perhaps 'jockeys' assistant' would be a more appropriate job description today, and we certainly rely on the men who perform that task. At the end of a day's racing we leave the valets with our breeches, boots, thin Lycra polo-neck sweater, which is worn under the colours, sweat jackets and towels, all of which are cleaned and ready for use the next day. Whether I've had six rides in thick mud at Newton Abbot or sweated buckets under hot sun at Bangor, my kit is always there when I need it, an invaluable service for which I pay £8 per ride. Valets are also the people we turn to for help with any emergency kit, an elastic band or safety pin or spare pair of breeches. That leaves me to take to the races my saddles – of which I have several of various weights – my lightweight breeches and boots, which I use when riding a horse near my minimum weight, my back-protector, crash-helmet, goggles, whip, medical book and the all-important tights which provide a little warmth while being very light in weight. And while we all carry our own saddles, because they would be too bulky for the valets to ship around the country, they clean them for us the moment we arrive at a meeting.

They are also the men who help us prepare for a race by taking charge of the colours which we wear to distinguish horses for the commentator and public. The colours are carried to the races by the trainer or travelling head lad and sent into the changing-room where the valet ensures the correct ones are hung on to the jockey's peg before each race. Valets also supply the lead which goes into a weight cloth under the saddle and which enables a person weighing 10st to ride a horse allotted, say, 12st.

No valet is better known than John Buckingham, a man who could probably walk down most streets in Britain without being recognised but who remains forever associated with one of the most remarkable sporting moments of the century – his victory on 100-1 shot Foinavon in the 1967 Grand National when all bar the winner were stopped, fell or were brought down at the 23rd fence. To watch film of the race now is still to wonder at the way Foinavon weaved through the mêlée and hopped over the jump, then hung on for victory as his remounted rivals galloped in vain pursuit.

That was definitely John's biggest win, and he knows from his own experience how tough this game can be so he is always very helpful to young lads coming into the weighing-room for the first time. They are nervous about the impending race and worry about having the right gear and making the correct weight but John takes them aside, kits them out and makes them feel like one of the lads. There's nothing worse than feeling like an outsider when you first step into a new institution.

John has looked after me since I came to England. He is always happy and goes about his work as though he is enjoying it. The weighing-room can be a depressing place when things go wrong and it is very easy to be tough on yourself in those conditions. John has experienced that and understands the pressure. He is always the first to ask if you are all right after a fall and if a jockey has to go to the ambulance room he takes on the job of checking on their condition, making phone calls on their behalf and arranging lifts home for riders who are feeling too poorly to drive.

He works around the southern and Midlands tracks with a team which mainly comprises his brother Tom, Andy Townsend and Shane Clarke. Any one of them will help, but I always rely on Andy, and occasionally John, to tie the coloured cap over my crash-helmet. Shane has never performed this task and while he does it perfectly well for other jockeys, superstition dictates in this instance. Racing and superstition might have been made for each other yet there is very little evidence of it in the weighing-room: you hear tales of jockeys who always pulled the right boot on before the left following a succesful ride, but in general we just get on with the job and try not to worry about whether the month has an 'R' in it or how many black cats have been in evidence. Jockeys could take superstitions to an extreme and since we are prone to falls and injuries, let alone getting beaten in races, riders would become nervous wrecks if they let their lives be ruled by such matters.

If I ride in the north another former jockey who has turned valet, Steve Charlton, takes over and supplies my kit while Dave Fox does the same job when I am in Ireland.

Racing is often accused of being backward but in one regard we must be leading other sports: mixed changing-rooms.

Women riders do have their own changing area but there are no women valets so if they want an elastic band or help with tying their cap to their helmet they have little option but to come into our changing-room. The more experienced women, those who get fed up hopping from one room to the other, virtually get changed with the men now, a trend which I remember Diane Clay starting at Aintree one year. Not only were all the valets in the men's changing-room, so too was the food, drink and colour telly, so Diane breezed in and there she stayed, starting a trend which others have followed and neither the men nor the women seem embarrassed.

Hywel Davies, a former colleague, felt differently. Now retired, he would go berserk when women walked into the changing-room, and I remember him getting uptight on one occasion with Gee Armytage. 'She wouldn't like it if I walked in while she was taking her clothes off,' ranted Hywel, and he had a point, but no one seems bothered now. By the time I have worried about beating the traffic, riding in races and remembering the details of the day there is no time to be concerned about whether a woman has seen my bits and pieces.

Diane became one of the lads, helped in part because she was a brilliant rider who had the respect of the weighing-room. I believe she was as good, and certainly as tough and hardy, as any man on her day. She was rare among women jockeys in that she had brute strength, a legacy of her body-building interest and a useful aid on occasions when all other forms of communication with a horse had broken down. Diane held her place among the jockeys because she was a good rider; her gender was irrelevant and while she is now retired from riding and works as assistant trainer to her father Bill, for me she remains the finest woman jump-jockey. Close behind would be Lorna Vincent, also retired now but a very good West Country-based rider in her day who enjoyed a lot of success while working for Mick Channon, the former footballer and now trainer. Sophie Mitchell is probably the best of the current crop, although she is small and light which tends to count against her. She has to carry a lot of lead-weight under the saddle, which in turn is dead-weight on the horse's back; it sits like a lump rather than moving in rhythm with the horse.

The debate about whether women get enough rides will probably rumble on for some time yet but the answer is quite simple: when a woman can blend in among the top male riders she deserves the same opportunities as them. Julie Krone, the brilliant American jockey, is constantly given as an example of what women can achieve; put her alongside the likes of Jerry Bailey, Mike Smith, Gary Stevens and Pat Day and Krone is their equal. I don't think that is true of any present-day women riders in Britain or Ireland and it seems many owners and trainers feel the same way. That is not to say women don't deserve rides and there have been countless occasions when a horse has won for a woman and no one doubts she was the decisive factor. Some horses simply run better for certain riders, of either sex, and if a woman jockey builds a rapport with a horse then they are the right person for the job.

Once we have weighed out we hand the saddle and number cloth to the trainer or their assistant who takes it away to place on the horse and we return to the weighing-room where I generally have a quick cigarette. We place coloured caps on top of our helmets which are tied tight by the valets and it is then simply a case of waiting for an official to walk in and say, 'Jockeys, please', a request which can take a while to produce any reaction if it's snowing a blizzard or raining hard outside. In those cases I pull on a pair of waterproof overtrousers but it can still be a pretty mucky business when the weather's bad.

We then head for the paddock, stopping to sign autographs if requested. We get asked regularly, especially at weekend meetings or when youngsters are on a day off from school, and I always try to fulfil requests for my signature, partly because it's a small way of doing something for the paying customers and partly from remembering the times when I was at school and wanted the autographs of sportsmen and women. There are times when it is impossible to take a pen wafted in my direction through the crowd, perhaps because I'm late or have to get changed for another race but most of the jockeys are happy to oblige.

There are many faces in the crowd which the jockeys recognise – the press corps makes itself known after each race while racegoers are a hardy bunch and you see people who you know travel all over the country for a day with the horses. Some are serious gamblers, others just like a flutter but they hate missing the action. One person who all the jockeys know is a tall, bespectacled chap called 'Dodger' – I don't know him by any other name – who is a great form man and when he says 'I think you'll have a good day today', it is a welcome sign. He has never asked me for information about the horses I ride and never criticised me either. That contrasts with another well-known racegoer, an elderly man who often attends Stratford and Worcester races and who must always back favourites, because if you are on one and it is beaten he stands near the exit from the track shouting and cursing you. Alternatively, if you oblige on a favourite he is all praise and regularly sends a pound coin into the weighing-room for the successful jockey.

We get on well with the media in general, taking the view they have a job to do and only getting offended if a derogatory comment paints us in a bad light. That would be true in any sport, but I do wonder sometimes whether a journalist has really understood what has taken place on the racetrack. I take an interest in all racing, flat and jumps, and I remember one comment about a horse which ran at Folkestone last year which said, 'given too much to do', meaning the jockey had left his challenge too late. I was at home that day and watching a video of the racing so I looked out for this horse, trained by Gary Moore who often gives me rides. There was no way the horse was given too much to do, he was simply outpaced.

When newspapers like the *Racing Post* or various other form publications give a 'comment-in-running' it really should mean that: a breakdown of the horse's run – not the opinion of the journalist. An analysis of a race is different, allowing for that opinion. Another issue which rankles with jockeys and which we raise with racecourse commentators from time to time, is their habit of adding unnecessary and unhelpful statements. Their job is to give the public a guide to the order of the horses while a race is in progress and it is annoying to hear a commentator add little extras such as a jockey has 'fallen off' when in fact the horse made such a blunder it was on its knees. Another common mistake in a tight battle is to say, 'and X's strength in a finish has won the day', insinuating that the other jockey has been outridden when in the vast majority of cases if you swapped the riders around the same horse would still win.

If asked, I always do my best to help the press out with interviews and while I don't expect any payment I do hope to be accurately quoted. This is generally not a problem but sometimes things you say can look quite damaging when they appear in print and that is not always the journalist's fault. If, in reply to a journalist's question, you say a horse was too slow, you might mean it was not fast enough on the day against its rival(s). That does not mean it is not honest and it could well pile up wins in the right grade or when it matures. Yet, when the horse's owner reads the comment in the papers the following day they could well be indignant. As a jockey you simply have to be careful about phrases you use when talking to the media, otherwise you can look very stupid or unsympathetic.

The quality and standard of riding among young jockeys is very high at present, which is so good for the sport because those standards perpetuate in the next crop of newcomers. They know they have to be fit, stylish, focused and sympathetic to horses if they are to take their place among the top jockeys.

These youngsters are often the trendsetters of tomorrow – one of them tries something different, perhaps mimicking a style they have read about or seen, and suddenly they are all doing it. The American Tod Sloan, who introduced riding with short stirrup leathers to Britain in the late 1890s, has gained his place in racing lore and further development in the American influence can be seen in flat racing today, most jockeys ride with just their toe in the stirrup and crouch very low in the saddle. When American jockeys Steve Cauthen, Willie Shoemaker and Cash Asmussen rode successfully in Britain their influence rubbed off, and with more and more British jockeys getting into races in the US and action from that country being given increasing coverage on television in Europe, young jockeys were bound to want to imitate the method. One moment we are like sheep, following the trend, the next we want to strike off and be an innovator. In the main we are sheep, influenced by our icons, and if Frankie Dettori crouches low with merely a toe in the iron, hordes of youngsters want to copy him.

For jump-jockeys such balancing acts using just the toe for

support in the stirrup are not recommended, although Paul Carberry briefly gave it a try to quite good effect after a fall left him with a bruised foot. For the rest of us the deceleration a horse makes when hitting a fence means that it helps to have the foot fully into the stirrup. Yet the way jump-jockeys ride today is influenced by flat racing, partly because it is effective and looks neat and partly because a number of us began by riding on the flat.

Taking nothing away from jump-jockeys of the past, I believe we are stronger and fitter than before and neater when it comes to riding a finish. The natural tendency to bounce around when galvanising a horse towards the line has been replaced by a rhythmical, streamlined style in which there is little lateral movement, and I would say that we are now as tidy in that respect as our flat counterparts. In the past it was not uncommon for people to point at jockeys who had ridden on the flat before turning to jump-racing, and say they had the edge in a driving finish, but I don't believe that is now relevant.

The reasons for the improvement are probably numerous, not least because of television coverage which means the vast majority of races in Britain can now be replayed again and again, a good lesson for youngsters who want to eradicate mistakes and tidy up their act and also repeatedly view the way top riders perform. Add to that a better understanding of fitness and dietary programmes, and a general raising of standards has been achieved as a result.

VII

Seven Barrows

Seven Barrows is home to my boss Nicky Henderson, his wife Diana, their three daughters, Sarah, Tessa and Camilla, some 90 to 100 horses and nearly 30 staff who make up one of the best racing stables in Britain. Named after the ancient burial mounds nearby, it is situated amid rolling downland in Berkshire about two miles from the village of Lambourn, an area known as 'The Valley of the Racehorse', a long-time base for racehorse trainers drawn there by springy turf on long gradient hills, ideal conditions for exercising thoroughbreds.

Before horses dominated the area, wool was the chief source of local income. The downs were ideal for farming sheep and fairs at Lambourn and West Ilsley drew herds from as far as the West Country. Dealers who bought stock at these market places would in turn take the animals to London. Seven Barrows was initially a sheep farm, a deep well making it an ideal place for keeping animals, but its potential as a base for racehorses was spotted by George Oates who became the first trainer there in 1862. Other trainers were to come and go and while it closed briefly as a training establishment before and during World War I it was put back on the racing map by Harry Cottrill, who saddled winners of the 2,000 Guineas (Adam's Apple) and Oaks (Lovely Rosa) while at the yard. Cottrill retired during World War II and while several other trainers tried their hand from the yard it became a major source of winners once Peter Walwyn took it on in the 1960s.

Training solely flat racers, Walwyn won the 1,000 Guineas with Humble Duty in 1970, the Oaks four years later with Polygamy and the Derby in 1975 with the flaxen-mane-and-tailed Grundy, whose subsequent thrilling victory over Bustino in the King George VI and Queen Elizabeth Stakes at Ascot is regarded as one of the races of the century. Walwyn topped up his portfolio with numerous big-race wins in Ireland and France and collected feature events at all the major meetings in Britain.

While Walwyn was enjoying hedonistic times at Seven Barrows, Nicky Henderson was enjoying a fair bit of success too, both as an amateur rider and assistant trainer to the legendary Fred Winter, one of the few men to head his profession both as a brilliant champion jockey and later as a trainer at the famous Uplands yard. Winter handled the careers of some outstanding horses, the quintet of Bula, Pendil, Crisp, Lanzarote and Killiney being champions all, even before you mention his Gold Cup winner Midnight Court. Nicky spent three years at the yard before taking out a licence of his own to train at Windsor Castle stables in Lambourn in July 1978, one month after marrying Diana Thorne, the daughter of John Thorne who owned and rode one of the best hunter chasers ever seen, the incredible Spartan Missile. Diana and her sister Jane also rode Spartan Missile in races, but it was John who formed the most successful partnership with the horse and together they mopped up all the top events in that sphere. In 1981 they finished fourth in the Cheltenham Gold Cup behind Little Owl and were second soon after in the Grand National when conceding 6lb to the winner Aldaniti. Tragically John Thorne was killed the following year while riding one of the family's young horses in a point-to-point.

Once set up in business, Nicky soon became established as one of the country's top trainers, saddling See You Then to win three Champion Hurdles besides picking up other big races with horses like Zongalero, The Tsarevich, River Ceiriog, Rustle and First Bout. He moved to Seven Barrows in 1992, swapping yards with Peter Walwyn who was looking to reduce the number of horses he trained and move to a smaller place. Nicky now has about 100 boxes at his disposal, some 400 acres of land, fabulous turf gallops which offer a choice of ground throughout the year, a curving uphill all-weather gallop which peels away from the yard, schooling hurdles and fences and a very useful oval-shaped indoor ride where the horses are warmed up each morning and can be kept on the move even if it is snowing. Large horse chestnut trees are dotted around the place, including one which towers over the centre of the main yard, and, convenient-ly, the Governor's house looks over the yard. This means he is on the premises in an emergency and it also means he can slip out at night to check a horse which is giving concern.

Over the rows of stable doors peer the horses, each one bedded down on straw, wood shavings or shredded paper. A natty, metallic-looking silver paint decorates the interior of the stables, not for aesthetic reasons but because it is anti-bacterial – keeping germs out requires vigilance – and each stable has two mangers, one for water, one for feed, while hay is placed on the floor. A chain hangs in each box for tethering the horses. It is a place which comes alive when the staff are present, usually between 7 a.m. and 1 p.m. and again from 4 p.m. to 6 p.m. Stable latches clank, brushes sweep, buckets are filled, hooves picked and horses led out, either for exercise under saddle or a session on the mechanical walker – a circular pen where they stretch their legs while on the easy list.

The Governor runs a successful yard, provides wages which match other trainers and offers good accommodation, either in a hostel for single staff or in cottages for married and senior members of the team. Yet he has an ongoing struggle to get good employees, a common problem for racing trainers across the country. You only have to look at the numbers of trainers adver-tising for staff, let alone hear general chat about the subject when visiting yards, to know that racing is finding it difficult to get and keep talented people working as grooms. Why this should be it is hard to say conclusively and while low wages are often blamed they have not suddenly slumped; in fact staff are now guaranteed a minimum agreed by the Stable Lads Association and the National Trainers Federation which includes bonuses for working Sundays and a share of the prize-money won by the yard.

Perhaps the problem has been created by the way we live today and our attitudes to careers. There was a time when people joined a company and stayed with it to work their way up the ladder but it is acceptable now to swap jobs without any stigma being attached. A person who has worked for Tesco, the general hospital, the local racehorse trainer, the pub, sports centre and McDonald's can boast a varied CV which some might see as a positive virtue. Our whole attitude to work has changed too. Machines make our lives easier but that has made us more accustomed to an easy life, whether it is changing channels on the TV with a remote control or using a washing machine to remove the boredom of standing at the sink. Yet racehorse maintenance has remained very demanding and with evening and Sunday meetings, summer jumping and racing overseas, it could be said that staff today have a more demanding job than their colleagues 50 years ago, even if they now have better living-quarters and proper wage schemes.

One other change in racing stables is the number of women now working in yards, often outnumbering the men, a ratio which would once have been unthinkable. This influx of women has been good for stables and without them it is hard to imagine many yards being able to operate. Yet this too can lead to a higher turnover of staff, a proportion of women leaving the industry each year because they marry or decide to start a family or because they simply do not retain the strength to go on doing such a physically demanding job into old age. Women are tough (how many males would be prepared to give birth!) but you don't see many in their forties, fifties and sixties working as stable staff. They seem to drift out of the job while lads who stay in it do so until they retire at 65. That means that if staff numbers are being held together by women, the average age is dropping and so too the level of experience.

You have to feel sympathy for women who would like to return to racing after giving birth but cannot pay for a nanny or childminder on the wages they earn, while if a woman and her partner decide to take on a mortgage she may be forced out of racing to seek a job which pays better money, even if it means leaving her beloved horses. Equality between the sexes may be getting closer but in a partnership it is still common for her career to be considered less important and if her wages are a good bit lower than his because she is working as a stable lass, it is not surprising that attitude prevails.

Trainers are in a difficult position – common business sense says that if you pay staff more money you have to get a higher price for the product you produce, yet asking owners to pay more is very difficult when their hobby is already expensive and there is competition for their patronage from other pastimes.

Yet the legacy of all these factors is that the standard of riding in stables is, I believe, lower now than it has been in the past. The level of care may be higher but there was a time when if a yard had 20 staff, almost all were capable of riding in races, and I don't think that is the case today, a remark which applies to the men just as much as to the women.

In general, though, stable staff do a fantastic job and their commitment is superb. The hours can often be unsociable yet you only have to look at the way most horses are turned out at the races, with manes and tails plaited and coats shining, to recognise the commitment away from the glamour of the race-track. Best-turned-out prizes which, as the name implies, are given to the groom of the horse which stands out in the parade ring, are very good recognition and a welcome bit of extra cash for lads and lasses who have often been up since before dawn, spent hours in a lorry travelling to a meeting and then rolled up their sleeves to make their horses look a picture of good health. Of course, professional pride says a groom would want their charge to look well, but it also does the British racing industry no harm and makes it so much easier for racing to talk about the way horses are given five-star treatment.

The staff all report to the head lad or lass, a senior position bestowed on a person with experience of riding all types of horses, of feeding greedy animals who devour the manger and finicky types who pick their way around individual oats, and with enough veterinary knowledge to heal cuts and bruises, administer injections and spot a horse with a troublesome tooth. The head staff usually live in a tied cottage adjacent to the yard, are first up in the morning to give the early feed and invariably last to finish if a horse has to be welcomed back from the races. They almost never go racing, as their job keeps them at the yard through good and bad times. Albert Browne, known throughout Lambourn as Corky, holds this position at Seven Barrows and both he and travelling head lad Johnny Worrall have been with the Governor since he started training more than 20 years ago. Talented people who are committed to racing in that way are vital.

Johnny, a former jockey, is known at racecourses up and down the country. As travelling head lad it is his job to transport the yard's horses to and from the racecourse, the sales or from other stables and studs. He is responsible for all the kit which is needed at the races, from the owners' colours, to the bridles, blankets and boots. All this is kept under lock and key in Johnny's glory hole, a cornucopia of supple, soaped leather, gleaming brass, steel bits and paddock sheets. Woe betide anyone who even thinks they might nip in and borrow an item because theirs has been mislaid. Johnny is small but his wrath is large.

He estimates that he drives 60,000 miles a year in his lorry, which is disinfected each time he moves a horse. At the races he is in charge of just about everything, stepping aside to let the Governor do the talking only when the horse is in the paddock. It is not unusual for Johnny to be responsible for six runners at a meeting and he has to remember which one wears boots, which one has bandages, which paddock sheet to put on and the type of bit for the bridle. The Governor's wife puts coloured ribbon on each browband to match the colours of individual owners, and Johnny recalls with embarrassment the day a lad picked up the wrong bridle at the start of racing and several horses subsequently ran with the wrong coloured browband. It was not his mistake, but he was responsible and you suspect he still feels it today.

Johnny rides out the same horse each day through the autumn until the number of runners means he is too busy to do so, and takes a particular pride in its fortunes through the season. He loves recounting the tale of how his father Jack, in company with a friend called Gordon, ran off while still school-boys to join a racing stables. Grandfather Worrall came after his boy and took him home to Birmingham but Gordon stayed as an apprentice and became perhaps the most famous jockey of them all, Sir Gordon Richards. Jack, his dreams dashed, was left to hope his son would be a jockey and Johnny fulfilled that wish – even though he did finish last in his first race after being thrown off his recalcitrant partner three times in the paddock!

At most modern yards there are assistant trainers, generally young people who have an ambition to train. Newmarket's Ed Dunlop, the son of former champion trainer John Dunlop, was once assistant to the Governor and his younger brother Harry now shares that role with Iona Craig. They ride daily and groom and feed when needed and they also get involved in some of the administration. If the Governor cannot be at a race meeting they go along as his representative, liaising with the jockey, greeting the owners and talking to the stewards or press if need be.

The lads and lasses each look after three or four horses and are responsible for mucking them out, riding and grooming them, feeding them hay and water and leading them up at the races. They eat in a staff canteen and many live on the premises. Not surprisingly among a group of people ranging in age from their mid-fifties down to school-leavers of 16 there is a fair bit of banter, the younger, cheeky ones regularly getting harangued by those who try to keep them in check.

Keeping staff happy in an outdoor industry where pay is relatively low and conditions often uncomfortable is very important and at Seven Barrows the staff rarely ride more than three lots. This is good for the employees and the horses who can be given more attention. I am not saying it is a holiday, but at least the staff have time to think. Most have worked at other yards and can tell tales of riding up to six lots, which means not stopping for lunch until well into the afternoon – and this while working for some very well-known and respected trainers.

Helping the operation run smoothly at Seven Barrows are a couple of yardsmen who look after three horses each but instead of riding ensure the yard is kept clean and muck out 'spares', those horses which are on the easy list or have yet to be allotted to one of the other members of staff. Not surprisingly there is much pride and a certain rivalry in looking after a good horse and if it is a comfortable ride, sensible on the gallops and not fazed by the antics of other horses then that is a real bonus. If you had to ride the same horse out for nine months of the year, on hot dusty days and cold ones when your fingers and toes are numb, you would hope it walks freely, trots purposefully and does not pull your arms out when asked to canter. What is to be avoided is some gassy creature whose walking pace is stationary one moment and galloping the next, who sees ghosts at every opportunity, who trots as though its knees have been placed back to front and who plunges and pulls like a demon on the gallops. A horse like that, day in and day out, is as much pleasure as surgery without anaesthetic and if it gets into a mucky, lather sweat which dries on the fur and takes hours to remove at evening stables, you have to be sympathetic to the member of staff. Tales of such horses and the devotion of their grooms often crop up in racing. Any bonuses the staff get, or tips from the owners, are richly deserved in such cases.

The team at Seven Barrows is completed by secretary Rowie Rhys-Jones who sorts out anything from wages to accounts and entries, a nanny called Rachel whose 'general dogsbody' role includes administering plasters to sick children and horses and cooking for owners, sundry other staff, occasional riders and gallops keepers, who harrow the all-weather training surface, maintain the schooling hurdles and fences and repair the turf gallops.

From my house at Faringdon I visit the yard three or four times a week to ride and school horses in preparation for the races. 'Work mornings', when horses due to run are given a decent gallop, take place on Tuesdays and Saturdays and I always attend on those days and whenever there are schooling sessions. My alarm rings most mornings at 6.45 a.m. and I am at the yard within half an hour, having dressed, cleaned my boots, had a cup of tea and a shave and collected the *Racing Post* from the newsagent. Some mornings it is tough getting up, particularly after a long drive the previous day, but it is always vital to arrive on time otherwise you are holding up the rest of the staff and, worse still, the trainer. Sometimes the shave has to wait, and although there has been the occasional sighting of a hirsute amateur – and former jockey Simon Earle once rode in a race while sporting a beard for charity – whiskers are not suitable for professionals. You sweat plenty in this job and the helmet strap would be uncomfortable against a bristly jaw.

My main obligation is to Seven Barrows, but I do ride in races for a number of trainers and if they need help with schooling horses I do my best to oblige, sometimes visiting them in mid-morning after riding out for the Governor and while on my way to a race meeting. Schooling horses can be critical, a horse which loses its nerve or develops bad habits while jumping at home is very difficult to put right. For that reason trainers want their stable jockeys to be available for such sessions, even if that means travelling hundreds of miles to a two or three-day race meeting, heading back for the following morning's schooling and then travelling back to the meeting for the next day's racing.

Once in the yard I make straight for the tack room to check a daily updated list informing those riding out which horses they are on, and then it is out to the boxes where I tack up my mount, put a quarter blanket on, that keeps the chill off the area behind the saddle, give them a brush over to flick any bedding off and pull out into the yard at 7.30 a.m. Being stable jockey to one of the premier yards in the country used to mean my horse was tacked up and led out by a member of staff but that perk faded away and I am sure there are more important things to do than wait on me. Once in the saddle we usually head for the indoor school where we walk our horses round while avoiding the worst of the weather and receiving instructions from the Governor – a traditional name which stable staff have long called their bosses. It probably seems dated in these times when even the office junior calls the managing director by their Christian name, but racing retains many links with the past and that is accepted. When addressing officials at the races such as starters and stewards we refer to them as Sir or Madam, which is a blessing since you don't want to be shouting 'No, Mr so-and-so', when the tapes are about to fly up at the start and your horse has suddenly turned sideways. As for the name 'Governor', it suits all occasions.

Unless the weather has rendered all hope of exercise futile, we ride out in rain, hail and shine. Five or six inches of snow does not stop us, although it might curb how far we go, and since the horses are in their boxes for some 22 hours a day it is important that we give them a chance to stretch their legs. There are times when it rains sideways and no amount of waterproof clothing can stop the rain running off our helmets and down our necks. Drowned rats could not look more abject but I try not to complain and instead feel sympathy for the staff who will be out in it again later while I am putting on dry clothes in readiness for the races.

At home – which in racing jargon means at the yard – all the staff wear helmets, a Jockey Club requirement which was brought in several years ago and upset some of the old school who had worn flat caps all their lives. Now, no one thinks twice before putting on their helmet. I carry a stick or whip and wear jodhpurs and black leather riding boots which come up to just below the knee and save any chafing of the calf, a very unpleasant experience as many riders will know. On wet days I put on a waterproof jacket and trousers and gloves and keep a pair of goggles on my helmet which can be pulled down to stop mud being flicked into my eyes when working in behind other horses.

Security and safety are evolutionary in all walks of life. We used to ride motorbikes without helmets and drive cars without seat belts, factory workers were exposed to noxious substances, miners would toil without masks while breathing filthy air. In racing, too, our ancestors exposed themselves to life-threatening dangers at a time when medical expertise was raw in comparison with today. Jockeys simply wore coloured silk caps on their heads and when helmets eventually came in after World War II, they were hardly good shock-absorbers and had no fastener under the chin, rendering them useless in many cases.

Today our helmets have to reach a certain standard before we can use them in races, while back-protectors, padded and giving protection to the whole of the upper body except the head, neck and arms, are compulsory. They fit around the chest and torso like a jacket but are still called back-protectors after the early models, a piece of dense polyfoam which gave limited coverage to the back. It tended to stick up and gave riders who were bending forward in the saddle the appearance of having a hump, not very flattering and often shunned for that reason. The modern version is far better and gives riders a rather muscular-looking physique, providing protection and flattery – there are no statistics on the effectiveness of body protectors in Britain but work done in France shows injury rates fell by nearly a third when they were introduced. Yet they are not compulsory when schooling at home. I suspect it is only time before that is changed.

At a seminar in the autumn of 1998 the Jockey Club's medical team recommended jockeys use back-protectors when schooling horses and it really is a bit daft to think we wear them in races on horses which should know the job, yet don't when jumping a young horse which may be getting off the ground for the first time. Part of the problem when trying to introduce the helmet was that those few riders who put it on were made to feel odd, as though they had something to be afraid of, and while such macho ridiculing is less common in all aspects of life today, it is still apparent. As far as back-protectors go, once Frankie Dettori, Tony McCoy and a few other role models turn up on the gallops wearing them, others will follow suit and we will wonder why we waited so long. People don't want to look like the Michelin man but it makes sense to stay in one piece, as Sean Curran, who punctured his liver while schooling, can vouch. Jockeys often turn up at the races limping or looking bruised after a fall on the gallops and there have been a couple of cases of stable staff being killed in accidents in recent years. A back-protector may not have saved them, but that does highlight the dangers.

Another safety device is the gumshield, which may one day become commonplace among jockeys but may not be so popular with stable staff – it would certainly make smoking a cigarette difficult. Warren Marston and Simon McNeill are but two jockeys who have tried gumshields, and while Jamie Osborne and Seamus Durack might both still have their front teeth had they been wearing one, a gumshield apparently also reduces the risk of concussion – when you fall on your chin or back of your head the impact of your lower jaw snapping shut creates an impact which can cause that condition and a gumshield would soften the blow in such cases.

It could also prevent a jockey biting their tongue or lip and might have helped me on one particularly unpleasant occasion when a horse trod on my face. I was riding at Sedgefield and took a fall on a horse called Safety, who unwittingly stood on my face as he got to his feet. I was aware of blood but could sense no pain, which was handy because when I put my tongue up to check my teeth were in place it went through a hole in my lip which was split from the base of my nose in a jagged tear. One small snippet of lip was the only thing holding it together and it took 14 stitches to repair the damage. I'll always have a slightly fat lip, although the scar would have been worse without some very fine work by the surgeon.

How I didn't lose teeth in that incident I don't know. I got even closer to a gap-toothed smile a couple of years later when riding a horse called Pashto, who threw his head up and caught me in the mouth, pushing a front tooth up through the gum. On that occasion I simply pulled the tooth down and worked it back into the hole from which it had been disturbed and luckily enough it took root again. A gumshield might have helped in both these incidents.

You don't have to be a scientist to realise that riding horses is dangerous, whether on the racecourse or in preparatory work at home, and thoroughbreds, who have been bred for speed, are as prone to moments of uncharacteristic behaviour as any breed. The fact that they get high-protein food and are trained to be fit and agile enhances the likelihood of them becoming unruly either through high spirits, fear and, occasionally, temper. The latter behaviour is rare as the horse is not an aggressive creature, but there have been cases of horses who become savage, probably because of mental illness which is almost impossible to detect, or a physical defect. Fortunately, such poor wretches don't reach the racecourse so jockeys have little dealings with them.

During the morning some three groups or 'lots' of horses will be exercised, usually numbering some 25 horses, each lot when out at exercise being known as 'the string'. Most of the staff ride three lots unless they have to leave early to take a runner to the races. The Governor often rides out with the first lot in the autumn, but as the days shorten racing starts earlier, so he monitors exercise from a jeep in order to save time, get finished earlier and get on the road for the races.

Occasionally a few horses will comprise a fourth lot. This often meant exercising horses on the easy list, but with staff shortages a trend has developed which means horses who are not in full work, because of injury or some other problem, are sent out to local livery yards where they recuperate before doing light exercise. My wife Jane runs just such a yard where she trains several point-to-pointers and looks after a few racehorses for local trainers.

My riding commitments at Seven Barrows centre solely on first lot, which usually means spending an hour and a half, sometimes longer, exercising and schooling horses. This is the most important lot because it comprises horses due to run in the next week to ten days who are undergoing the fine tuning which leads up to the race. Second lot normally contains horses due to run in two to three weeks' time while third lot probably consists of horses which have just run and are therefore having an easy few days before stepping back into full exercise. But that is only a general guide because some horses, perhaps those who get excited or are temperamental, are only ever ridden by certain riders and therefore have to wait until that rider is free. Quite often pairing a certain member of staff up with a horse can improve that animal, particularly if it is shy, temperamental or headstrong. A person who can bring out the best in such horses is worth their weight in gold and much sought after.

The horse I ride out of the yard may not carry me back since schooling over jumps can mean getting on and off several horses. Once this is completed it is back to the yard where the staff take a 30-minute break for breakfast in the canteen. This break is skipped on Saturdays so that everyone can get to their homes for the start of televised racing. Staff hate missing a race on the box in which there is a runner from their yard, particularly if they have had a bet on it!

Meanwhile, I check running plans for the horses with the Governor over a cup of tea in the office and he tries to assess the likely opposition, often by a quick call to my agent. As I mentioned in an earlier chapter, there is a growing number of freelance jockeys but these early-morning team talks are an example of the benefit of a stable jockey, one who rides a trainer's horses on a regular basis at home and on the racecourse, and is on hand to give an appraisal of likely winning opportunities.

I never ride a second lot, my next job being to get home and prepare for the day's racing, a fairly leisurely event if a meeting is local, but an exercise in clock-watching on many days of the week. If I am home from Seven Barrows by 9.45 a.m. and have to travel to Doncaster, which is two and three quarter hours away, then the earliest I can reach the course is 12.30 p.m. If the first race is at 1.15 p.m. there is precious little time to spare and occasionally, if racing is starting earlier, I have to skip riding out and go straight to the course.

VIII

On the Gallops and at the Track

When it comes to riding in races the first advice I would give to a novice is: keep it simple.

Many of the world's greatest sportsmen and women have adhered to that principle, rarely reaching for the extravagant, and you only have to think of some great footballers, players who perform at the highest level over many seasons, to witness stars whose game is simple but commanding. They retain control of the ball while putting the opposition under pressure. In the weighing-room that message is often the root of advice handed out by senior jockeys to young riders. It is not uncommon to hear a forlorn youngster asking, 'What should I have done?'

The stock reply in most cases is, 'You should have done nothing – keep it simple and let the horse sort itself out.'

My job is to get the best from a horse each time it runs and, assuming they are fit and well and have conditions in their favour, my first priority is to sit quietly and be in the right place at the right time – where that is depends on the number of runners, the pace of the race, the course and the opposition. There is rarely a hard-and-fast rule that can be given as to where a rider should be at any one time in a contest, so you have to be adaptable. What a jockey can do in advance is work upon the natural talent they have been given in the same way that a professional piano player would practice to produce smoother and more intricate playing. More practice means better, smoother execution in the saddle, but there must be natural talent too – and if you have not got it you probably have no wish to sit on a horse in the first place, let alone ride in a race. People can be taught to ride but that does not mean they will ever be good jockeys, others can be taught to play piano but will never perform in a concert at the Proms.

Good race-riding begins both at a jockey's home and at the yard where the horses they ride are prepared. It is there that an aspiring jockey shows his mettle and convinces a trainer to give them a ride in a race, but it is also where young horses are educated and in that respect a senior jockey has plenty of work to do, riding and schooling novice horses so they have a good idea of what is required when reaching a racecourse. It can be a real chore on cold, wet days in winter when it is no fun leaving the warmth of the stables for the bleakness of the gallops, but it can pay off handsomely.

Horses differ in shape and size and the amount of work they require to bring them to race fitness depends on the individual. A really good 'doer', one who eats with relish and gets fat within a few days of being in a field, will take longer to get fit at the start of the season than a fussy horse which spends half its time looking around and merely nibbles at its food. Yet the principle is the same and while the severity of the training grounds, for instance the gradients and length of a trainer's gallop, will determine how much work a horse should be asked to do, getting them fit involves starting slowly and building up the work.

Most jumping horses get a holiday from the job at some time of the year and they benefit from having a month or two out in a field, particularly in the spring and early summer when the grass is at its peak and before the weather gets too hot. Those horses who race through the summer will get their break at a different time but the theory is the same: give the horse a chance to unwind and replenish its interest in the job. Once the holiday is over the campaign to get them back on the track will begin with about four weeks of walking and trotting, generally on roads. Many owners choose to do this part of the job themselves and if they have the facilities at home it adds to the fun of owning a racehorse. If a horse is particularly gross or has been on the easy list for a long time because of injury this period of work could be extended. The next stage is cantering.

At Seven Barrows an all-weather gallop nearly three-quarters of a mile long and made of a sand and rubber mix, which drains well but has a bit of bounce, is the ideal place to begin this faster work. There is very little 'kick-back' (material thrown up by the horse in front) and it can be used, as its name implies, in just about all weathers. The gallop, which is harrowed by a tractor after each lot, rises about 150 feet, a good test which makes a horse work without breaking their resolve.

Once horses are ready to use this gallop they canter up it once, in Indian file with the rest of the string, perhaps being allowed to trot from halfway if they find it hard going. They will be kept to this level for a week to ten days and it is really then just common sense which dictates how quickly you press on. Once a horse is cantering to the top of the gallop in one go it will be asked to do so twice, kept at this level for a couple of weeks and then asked to canter three and finally four times. There are some horses which simply don't like the all-weather gallop, perhaps because they find it too tough or have hamstrings which pull on the surface, and they are kept on the grass gallop.

The next stage is a spin on the grass, generally at a faster pace, a 'swinging canter' as it is known, which means letting the horse extend into the gallop while still keeping a firm hold of their head by simply keeping the reins taut. Horses will perform this gallop in twos or threes, in one line abreast or one tucked behind the other two. This is where a young horse learns the first lessons about racing – putting them in behind other horses gives an impression of what it is like to be galloping while the hooves and mud are flying in front. You can imagine how daunting it would be for young horses, who have only ever galloped on their own or have always led their companions, to find themselves jammed in among 15 or 16 other horses in their first race; that could cause a mental block in many animals.

The final stage in this fitness regime is known as 'a pipe-opener' which is normally given to a horse a day or two before it runs. After setting off at a good pace the horse is urged to extend for a few furlongs, which blows the cobwebs away and opens its windpipe. Neither human nor animal is going to win a race if they have congestion in their airways. However, a pipe-opener is not like a race, the riders do not draw their whips or kick and shove, although a very lazy horse might be cajoled rather more vigorously than a free mover. A nice contact through the reins is always maintained to encourage the horse to hold itself together. If it begins galloping too freely it could injure itself, perhaps through stumbling or striking into its front legs with the back hooves (known as an overreach), or worse. Breaking down means acute lameness through an injury to the tendons or ligaments which run from behind and below the knee to the fetlock, or because of a fracture to a bone. The tendons in a horse's front legs take a lot of strain, particularly when landing over a jump, and if there is a weakness they can become stretched or ruptured. The usual signs are lameness, heat and puffiness; tendon injuries are a thing which all trainers dread.

Horses which have broken down can be cured – some are simply given a year to 18 months in a field, while others can be given a range of veterinary treatments, including firing, blistering and carbon fibre implants. These options are carried out under anaesthetic and the first two are designed to produce scar tissue and swelling around the injury so that blood can flow freely to it and help repair the damage. Blistering involves the application of a cream which irritates the skin while firing involves placing a hot iron into or around the area of the injury. Some vets swear by both methods, others feel they are unnecessary. In general they work well and some people say a horse which has been fired has tougher tendons than one which has not been treated. That may be true, but a horse which has broken down is generally treated with added caution.

Trainers differ in how often they work their horses and how far. Terrain is a factor, a gallop which is relatively flat is less testing than one on the side of a hill. The modern trend towards 'interval training' means that horses tend to do four- to six-furlong canters, between half and three-quarters of a mile, several times, rather than long pieces of work, which was the fashion in the past. Tales of horses galloping for four and five miles across heathland the day before winning a major race are commonplace in books which look at the history of racing, but an unthinkable preparation these days, although horses do still run in races on consecutive days and often perform well.

Interval training developed and expanded with the introduction of all-weather gallops which are expensive to install and maintain – keeping them relatively short makes financial sense and reduces the time it takes to harrow or roll them after use. Variations on the theme include: peat, sand, cinders or woodchips. These have been in use for many decades and trainers based on the coast have long used beaches, a surface which did Red Rum no harm on his way to winning three Grand Nationals.

The problem with the early all-weather gallops was drainage – they were often put down straight onto the ground and could get very wet in winter. Their main purpose was to give a surface for working on in a freeze when the turf became like concrete. Modern all-weather gallops are far more versatile and drain well because they are laid on a membrane which allows water to seep away. These surfaces are now used all-year round, providing a surface with some give in dry summers and frozen winters and, very importantly, saving grass gallops from getting chewed up.

Martin Pipe and Paul Nicholls are but two trainers who only use an all-weather surface, but at Seven Barrows the quality of the turf, long established, springy and quick-draining, means that we have the best of both worlds. Given the choice, a grass gallop is still best for doing fast work on because it is natural, consistent and the surface on which the horse will be asked to race, but Pipe and Nicholls prove it is not essential.

Pipe, an innovative thinker who loves finding ways of winning races, is credited with the modern-day method of interval-training for racehorses after he installed a short all-weather gallop on his land near Wellington in Somerset. Yet other trainers were doing the same thing with their horses long before he came on the scene, the difference being they used a bank or short hill simply because it was available and near their yard. They did not realise they were forerunners in using a method which is now followed almost religiously. It was only Martin Pipe's incredible list of achievements, helped by a very large string of horses, which brought the method to a wider audience.

Schooling is the business of teaching young horses, and reminding older horses, how to jump. Some experienced horses seem to loathe this process and make a real pig's ear of it, jumping awkwardly and even breaking hurdles and fences, yet leaping fluently at the racetrack. It is a futile exercise trying to school such horses at home and many never jump a twig other than in races from one year to the next. Other older horses love jumping and make ideal 'leads', combining a useful racing career with leading young horses over jumps, the idea being that the youngster will learn from the master. This job is sometimes given to ex-racehorses and the 1991 Cheltenham Gold Cup winner Garrison Savannah, who is still with trainer Jenny Pitman, is one who carries out this role.

Before the youngster arrives at the stage where it follows a lead horse, most of the novices from Seven Barrows are sent to Lars Breisner, known throughout the horse world as Yogi. A former event rider, based in Oxfordshire but who represented Sweden in the Olympics, Yogi has now turned his hand to tutoring horses and humans in jumping. Whether teaching young horses or correcting bad habits in older animals, he does an excellent job. Some trainers shun him, preferring to do the job themselves, and if they have staff who have the time and are capable, all well and good. Yet Yogi is a specialist and therefore picks up little things before most other people. In times of staff shortages it also suits many trainers in the Lambourn area to use him, leaving their staff free to do routine work. Working with a problem horse can be very time-consuming.

At Yogi's the young horse begins by walking and trotting over coloured showjumping poles which are gradually raised in height. This went against the grain when it was introduced, some traditionalists saying young hurdlers and chasers should jump the type of obstacles they would find when racing, not showjumping poles which they can knock over. Breisner maintains that it is not the type of jump which counts, it is the way in which the horse jumps, and since poles can be raised or lowered easily they suit his purpose. Once horses have been through his hands and returned to Seven Barrows we then put them over little hurdles in our own indoor school where the lesson in getting from A to B continues and they seem far more efficient when it comes to jumping over full-size hurdles on the schooling grounds at racing pace in company with other horses.

I really don't understand why people criticise Yogi or question his role – I can only surmise his critics have never used his services which I have found are wholly beneficial, and I speak from the experience of having had a lesson from him; it is not only horses he teaches – many jockeys, young and old, have benefited from a lesson. Within a few moments of observation he can spot an area in which the rider could improve their man-to-horse co-ordination and in my case he felt I was a little too busy in the saddle. He suggested I simply sat a little quieter and used my hands, legs and upper body less. This is not to say I was riding in an all-action style but Yogi felt a subtle change, almost impossible to spot by someone who had never ridden, would be an improvement and I had to agree with him. Using videos of races he is also happy to analyse both a jockey and the horse they are riding. It can help to get a second opinion and in Yogi's case he is detached from the horse and unbiased. He is also a very pleasant, fair-minded person who has never claimed to be a special talent or guru as the press have labelled him, and, to my knowledge, he does not tell people they are doing something wrong unless specifically asked for his view.

Horses from Seven Barrows are some of the best schooled in racing and may jump up to 60 hurdles before they are asked to make their debut in a race. At the schooling grounds, in a field just across the road from the yard, there are four flights of hurdles and fences, wide enough to get several horses jumping in line abreast if needed, and here practice makes perfect. You would not want to sicken a horse by asking it to jump every day and those who do the job naturally will have fewer lessons – eventually it comes down to the Governor deciding when he feels a horse has done enough and is ready to race.

In many cases that first test will be in a bumper or National Hunt flat race, a contest without jumps and from which horses who have run in flat races are excluded. The purpose of a bumper is to give potential jumpers a taste of going to the track, experiencing the sights and sounds and being asked to gallop among a group of strange horses without the burden of having to think about jumping. It is a gentle introduction.

Next step is a novices' hurdle, in which the youngster gets a chance to compete against rivals of similar experience but has to jump hurdles in the process. A few horses, perhaps those who are on the big side, slow maturing and therefore too weak to race over hurdles at four and five, may make their racecourse debut in a chase, jumping birch fences. While hurdles have to be a minimum of 3ft 6ins (about 107cm), fences must be no less than 4ft 6ins (about 137cm) and, height apart, the two obstacles are quite different from each other. Hurdles are made of wooden frames with gorse woven through them. They are driven into the ground but give or fall flat when rapped by a horse. Fences, which in past centuries would have been natural hedgerows, are made of birch, tightly packed into a wooden frame and to a depth at the top of about 15ins to 20ins (38-50cm) which is given a sloping cut so as not to look too upright. Supposedly uniform around the country, they are decidedly stiffer and more testing on some courses than others, which does at least give trainers the chance to pick and choose a chase to suit the experience of their horses. However, very soft fences can lead a young horse to think it can brush through the top of the birch, which would be a mistake once it races at a course with stiffer fences.

Schooling over fences requires experience and a rider would need to be proficient over hurdles before attempting the bigger jumps. At Seven Barrows we have a row of three baby fences, which gives the young horse a chance to realise they are jumping something which does not give, and a row of four full-size fences. Experience soon tells a rider whether a horse is likely to jump a fence smoothly or awkwardly, depending on their stride as the fence approaches. This is known as being on the right or wrong stride, a reference frequently made by jockeys when talking about races. They often say, 'I saw a good stride and he came up for me', meaning the jockey could spot the best place for take-off and the horse responded too. If the take-off point, say one and a half metres from the fence, is exactly six strides away, a jockey can be reasonably sure that in six strides' time the horse will get airborne. If the horse's stride means its front hooves are going to land just before the ideal take-off point, say two metres away from the fence, it means one of two things: the horse is either going to have to take off early and stretch for the landing side, or put in another stride, get in close to the fence and cat-jump.

Really good jumpers get so good at the business they will

shorten or lengthen their stride accordingly as they approach a fence and what a thrill it is. There is nothing better in a day's work than to ride such a horse.

Trainers have different ideas about schooling over fences but the Governor likes to see horses going at a sensible gallop, so the horse has enough impulsion to make a good jump but not going so fast that it has little time to think. Schooling sessions generally start at a steady pace and get a little quicker as a horse improves, so for its last school before running in a race it's jumping at about racing pace.

In these lessons the horse is encouraged to quicken as the fence approaches and once on the other side is steadied again before the process is repeated at the next fence which is some 30 to 40 yards (27–36 metres) away. On the other hand the horse should be going steadily enough so that if it is on the wrong stride it has time to sort itself out in order that it gets to the other side in one piece. Sometimes this involves an untidy, rather flat-footed jump, but the idea is that the horse should learn from the experience and not be frightened by it. If you are going flat out in these schooling sessions the horse can only make two sorts of jumps: a very brave one or a complete horlicks – and if they end up on the floor, which does happen at even the best yards on occasions, it can take time to rebuild confidence.

If a horse develops a phobia about jumping you have to retrace your steps and that can mean going back to jumping over little poles. Lesser cases might simply have to be given some sessions over fences on their own, so they are concentrating purely on jumping and not worrying about other horses. When schooling over fences we begin by putting a youngster behind a lead horse who shows the way and encourages the novice to follow. Then two horses, side by side, lead the youngster, who obviously can see less of the fence ahead. In this situation they learn to jump as if in a race, and it is noticeable how experienced jumpers can take off blindly when they need to – it is their skill and again illustrates why it is better to keep it simple and let the horse sort itself out.

Being led over fences by other horses usually achieves satisfactory results but some horses are forever clumsy in this situation and yet jump boldly and athletically when allowed to do the leading themselves. I cannot tell you why this happens, but an experienced rider and trainer can spot this type of horse and give it the chance to try leading before confidence is spoilt. Experience really can make a difference at these schooling sessions, and in that regard I thoroughly enjoy the job when working alongside Johnny Kavanagh, who is number two jockey at Seven Barrows. A really competent rider who is naturally keen to make the most of any chances that come his way, Johnny is also a very good ally and work colleague. He and I take part in almost every schooling session at Seven Barrows and have built up an understanding. Once the Governor has told us which horses are going to jump and whether he would like them leading or sitting in behind, Johnny and I go onto auto-pilot – we rarely ask what sort of pace the other wants, we rarely have to discuss how far behind the other person wants to be. It is all done very smoothly and means that we concentrate on the horse we are riding.

Not that these sessions are 100 per cent successful and we had to admit defeat with a good horse a year or two back. Barna Boy, a very fast two-mile hurdler, had the ability to compete for an Arkle or Queen Mother Chase but after winning a novices' race over fences at Leicester, jumping adequately while getting a bit low at some of the jumps, he completely lost the plot and subsequently demolished more fences on the schooling grounds than any horse in Lambourn. No end of practice and searching for clues could solve the problem and his jumping became so ropey that we had to admit defeat. Back over hurdles he won the County Hurdle at the Cheltenham Festival but we feel he could have attained a far higher grade as a chaser.

Whether preparing to canter or work a horse, school it or go to the start for a race, riders should avoid getting their partner geed up. Once in that state it can take a long time before they calm down, which makes them unpleasant to ride, apt to getting loose and could cost them a winning chance in a race. Some very idle horses do need to be stoked up a little, but in most cases the thoroughbred needs no invitation to gallop, especially when their mates are doing likewise. When riding a hard-pulling or nervous horse riders should ease them into the canter, rather than take off as though the posse is in pursuit. The reins and bit and the contact with the horse's mouth are crucial aspects.

When the horse walks naturally it extends its head and neck forward. At the trot the neck contracts and the head comes up, which means that to have the same contact with the mouth and to avoid the reins becoming slack between the rider's hands and the bit, the reins have to be shortened. When the horse canters, its neck shortens again, although at the gallop the neck is lowered and extended. Novice riders make the mistake of grabbing the reins closer to the bit when the horse is about to break into the canter, which is okay on a riding school, bomb-proof horse but asking for trouble on a thoroughbred. Doing so can ignite a racehorse as quickly as if someone had flailed them with a whip and it is often best to loosen your grip and give strong horses extra rein, encouraging them to relax and reducing their urge to battle. Giving extra rein to a big strong horse which is pulling hard goes against human instinct to pull against the thing which is pulling, but I can assure you it works.

The secret to avoid a confrontation, hard though it is to convey to the novice, is to slide the hands gently down the reins as the horse picks up to go into the canter. The more sensitive the horse, the more sensitive this manoeuvre must be, and in some cases you can kid the horse that they are not really cantering by remaining seated in the saddle, perhaps only for a few strides until the horse settles, rather than standing up in the stirrups which is a signal to the racehorse that cantering is under way. People ask why jockeys ride with shorter stirrup leathers than riders in other forms of equestrianism, standing out of the saddle with a slightly bent knee when cantering and galloping. The aim is to put yourself as far as possible over the horse's shoulders where they carry weight better than in the middle of their back. The saddle still has to be fastened to the horse with girths in the traditional place but by getting forward the rider is helping the horse gallop and making themselves as light as possible. You can crouch down and make yourself streamlined in this position.

Experienced jockeys and stable staff rarely get run off with as they can sense trouble coming, often by the expression in the horse's eye or its body language which is more animated when they are nervous or excited. At the races that means getting into the saddle as quietly as possible and if the horse immediately begins jogging or threatens to shy I take hold of the mane or the neck strap (part of an elasticated breast-girth, a device which attaches to the saddle and is placed around the chest of the horse to keep the saddle from slipping back) and leave my feet dangling by the side of their body as horses often work by association and if experience tells them that shortly before galloping riders gets their feet into the stirrups and shortens the reins then any sign of those movements can induce a quickening in tempo. To defuse that thought you want to do the opposite. You are not only trying to ensure you don't get hurt, you are also trying not to alarm the horse. The last thing you want is for them to have a horrible experience and be thinking at a later date, 'Oh my God, I remember this. It was horrendous. I'm not going through this again.'

By applying calming measures and using the voice to make soothing tones, the experienced rider can generally keep the situation more or less under control. You do see jockeys suffering occasionally and I have been bucked off in the paddock on more than one occasion, while the grisly business of being run off with, sometimes in a race but more generally going to post, is not pleasant. It happens when the keen horse simply wants to get on with the job and the rider is trying to conserve energy and keep it calm.

Several tricks can be used in a bid to get a headstrong horse to the start and, bearing in mind that the sight of other horses galloping is usually the catalyst for any fireworks, severe cases often go to post early while their rivals are still walking around the paddock. Jamming the hard-pulling horse up the backsides of other rivals is something you see occasionally when a jockey is in danger of getting run away with but it is not something I would advocate because it can lead to injury if the front hooves of the tearaway clip the hind legs of the horse in front. It is better to go down to the start very slowly and I usually tell the lad or lass leading the horse out of the paddock to let go so that I am in sole control before I ask my partner to canter. Talking to the horse and quietly saying 'whoa, whoa', is also a good way of keeping the situation calm. Once out on to the course I just let the horse trot a little way and then move into a lobbing canter. If their head is tucked into their chest all the better, because that gives me pressure upon the bars of the mouth, the gaps in a horse's jaw between the front and back teeth where the bit sits. On the other hand if my horse lets me know they would like a little more rein by flicking their head and tugging at the bit, I let them have just enough so that they are happy but I still retain control. A happy horse will soon settle. The scenario you want to avoid is the horse which gets into a gallop, the pace at which its neck extends, and then fights against the bit by putting its head in the air, so that the rider is pulling not against the bars of the mouth but the cheeks, and while you might assume that would slow a horse down, it doesn't – you might as well be pulling on its tail.

One incident, on the way to post at a Cheltenham April meeting, demonstrated how easily the rider can lose the battle if the horse decides to use its strength. I was riding the Queen Mother's horse Kings Rhapsody, only five and immature, who had become increasingly headstrong in the days before the race, partly because he was getting fitter through racing and partly because he was getting clued up to the excitement of going to the races. While I was aware of this and did my best to keep him from boiling over he took a strong hold as we went to post. The route to the start at Cheltenham involves going downhill past the grandstands, so a keen horse has not only the noise of the crowd and the bookmakers to gee them up, it also has gravity helping it gather speed.

Adding to the likelihood that he would become excited were the 21 other runners, lots of fun for a youngster, but I countered this by going down first, just ahead of a group of other horses, which meant my fellow had only a wide space to look at, keeping him reasonably sensible. We had just about got to the start when Andy Thornton came flying past on another headstrong horse and that was it: lighting-up time! Whoosh – Kings Rhapsody took off as though someone had put a banger up his backside and the next moment I was being carted (Andy managed to pull his horse up soon after). Normally the rider acts as a brake but in this instance I was as much use as a handkerchief on a car aerial and despite using all my strength it made not a scrap of difference. I mentioned earlier that you can kid a horse to relax by giving it more rein and by not pulling against it, but when they are in full-scale bolting mode that will not work. At least I could steer him so decided, as we flew up the hill going the reverse way around the famous course, to turn right and down towards the start, which began in the centre of the track – this while travelling at the flat-out gallop on a horse which would probably tank through a brick wall. There have been some sad cases of runaway horses doing just that, with fatal consequences. We continued haring down the middle of the course when I realised some double plastic rails would be ahead round the corner. Plastic rails are not as dangerous as brick walls, but they are still pretty solid and could bring the horse down, which at that speed would not be nice. 'I'll turn on to the old course,' I thought to myself, and with Kings Rhapsody taking the corner on two wheels, we took a sharp turn right and were now heading in the general direction of the distant grandstand. This was a long stretch of grass and I reasoned he would probably stop tugging at some point, but horses can make fools of you and if anything he got stronger and quicker while my arms became weaker and my strength evaporated to the consistency of pasta. Worse still, another set of plastic rails lay ahead.

At this point I had three options: shutting my eyes and praying, bailing out or setting him up to jump the rails which were about five foot high, not huge but we were supposed to be taking part in a bumper race and I wasn't even sure this horse could jump. There was not much time to think so I set him up, saw a stride and asked him to take off. Crash! He completely ignored me and smashed straight through the rails, shocking himself so much that he stopped virtually immediately. I managed to remain in the saddle and while the journey from hell had ended I was hugely relieved to find he was completely unmarked. Not surprisingly we withdrew from the contest.

The alternative to that episode is the horse which is 'cold-blooded' and needs a brisk gallop to get warmed up before a race. If a trainer tells me their horse is this type I will encourage it to stride out on the way to post and may go a few hundred yards past the start before turning and cantering back. Each horse is different and, while we generally ride horses at home before partnering them in a race, there are occasions when we sit on them for the first time at the course. Any advice the trainer can give is welcome but I always give the horse the benefit of the doubt and assume they are well mannered and know the job. If it proves otherwise I have to adjust as we go along and try to pick up their nuances quickly.

At the start we all have our girths checked, ensuring they are tight enough to prevent the saddle slipping, which can happen when a horse stretches its body to leap a fence, and then keep on the move until the starter calls us into line.

Races often start at a pretty quick pace these days, especially if Martin Pipe has a runner. So you have to be alert, not chatting to a colleague about last night's film or daydreaming about winning. You do not want to concede ground unnecessarily at the start, even if you intend tucking in near the back of the field, and if you are on a genuine and nimble horse you are lucky because you will be able to grab a good position and get away smoothly when the starter says go. A jockey has a far more anxious time on a slow starter in a big field – that could mean going over the first fence virtually blind – while the horse which stands still at the start, 'planting' themselves, can be a real headache. Some horses perfect this habit and become unraceable rogues, while others will jump off some days but not others. A skilful jockey can make quite a difference with such horses, convincing them the job will be fun or kidding them they are not on a racecourse.

The trick most commonly used with such horses is to keep them on the move, often trotting them around at the start – horses which are thinking of digging their toes in are less prone to do so while on the move yet once they stop that is their cue to become permanently stationary. The jockey's next challenge is to get the reluctant beast to 'jump off' – to start as soon as the lights turn green and that can mean trotting them in towards the starting tape. This has to be timed with precision so that the horse is moving forward but not so fast that the starter decides you are getting an unfair advantage. Getting your time wrong means you have no option but to stop your horse or risk colliding with the tape – stopping the horse means they plant themselves and the battle has been lost, which is very frustrating. There is often little you can do; my only advice is stay calm and try not to let the horse know you have just been thwarted but try to get them on the move by turning away and trotting round before coming in again. The starter will almost certainly be aware of your predicament and they invariably do their best to help while avoiding accusations of unfairness.

From that point on, the tactics you employ in the race will depend on the trainer's instructions and how the horse is best ridden. If riding a youngster I prefer to tuck in behind the leaders where my horse will learn about racing in a group and, with luck, can pass a few rivals in the closing stages, but there are no firm rules. If the horse is settled I try to ensure it has a bit of room over the first couple of jumps, easing myself down into the saddle a couple of strides from the hurdle or fence and relaxing my grip on the reins. If the horse is pulling hard it is still important to relax your grip because it has to extend its neck to jump and if you keep a tight rein you will be jerked forward while at the same time jagging your partner in the mouth. Any slight mistake on landing could end up with you being pulled over the horse's head, and if they fall you will be pulled into the ground – a likely way of breaking your neck or back. Holding the reins too tightly and too close to the bit is a mistake common among novices, particularly, it seems, in point-to-points, where some very callow youngsters learn about race-riding; not surprisingly, the injury rate in points is higher than in races under Rules. Slipping the reins and giving a horse freedom of its head is one way of avoiding injury and while it is hairy as hell to ride a bolting horse with its head stuck in the air and instinct dictates that you want to pull on the reins, the sight of the fence normally makes a horse think about jumping and it is better to relax your grip, which will also enable you to let the reins slip through your fingers if the horse pitches on landing. With practice you will find that you know before take-off whether a horse is likely to jump smoothly and you will automatically get in the appropriate position. If the horse is likely to pitch on to its nose on landing you need to be sitting back against the deceleration, if the horse is about to make a smooth jump you want to remain sitting forward so that you can help it continue with the gallop on the landing side and not have to wait while you bounce about in the saddle and gather up the reins.

The alternative to the hard puller is the horse which seems to be lacking in confidence and does not jump with enthusiasm. On such horses you should still adhere to the tenet which says keep them balanced by sitting quietly and maintain a nice length of rein, but you should also urge them forward as the fence approaches by sitting a little deeper in the saddle and pushing through your torso – that does not mean kicking them in the belly or hitting them, which is likely to make them less confident. If gentle urging fails you may have to be more vigorous, by giving them a slap with the stick, initially down the shoulder while keeping hold of the reins and then behind the saddle if you still get no response. The reason a horse jumps poorly, physical problems apart, is because they are nervous or bloody-minded about racing and you have to decide which it is and what is the best option, either cajoling and sympathetic urging, or discipline in a bid to prove who is boss. As the golfer Gary Player once said, 'The more I practise the luckier I get.' While it would be nice to teach novice riders how to jump thoroughbreds at racing pace before they get on the track the only way really to grasp the issue is to take part in a race.

That applies also to use of the whip, a controversial implement, vital to jockeys on many occasions, but a curse upon racing if used incorrectly or excessively. Prior to the publication of this book the RSPCA had threatened to prosecute jockeys for whip misuse which, if it happened, could seriously damage racing's image. To ensure that does not happen and, more importantly, to gain good use of the whip in a way which does not harm a horse, you should treat it as something which is only to be used when really necessary. If your horse has jumped well, gone to the front and is cantering to victory, you have no need to use the whip. However, if there are at least two of you in with a chance of winning there will come a point when you have to start riding more vigorously. Initially, this should be done by lowering your bottom nearer the saddle so that you can put pressure behind your hands and at the same time squeeze with your legs and lower body. In addition I like to change the position of the reins in my hands by shortening them, a sign to the horse that I would like it to go faster. Frankie Dettori, the brilliant flat-race jockey, is a master of this and he uses it very effectively. Watch him on film and you can clearly see him pulling the reins sideways away from the horse's neck, sliding one hand down the reins, and then repeating the manoeuvre and sliding the other hand down. This movement sends a signal to the horse that more speed is needed and on this shorter rein he can then extend his arms and hands forward up the horse's neck while still retaining contact with its mouth, a loose rein in most cases meaning, 'Okay, you can slow down now, the race is over.' I would just add here that jockeyship is an individual craft and both Kieren Fallon and Adrian Maguire, one a top-notch jockey riding on the flat and the other fantastic over jumps, defy the convention which says you should keep some contact with the horse's mouth. When driving for the line and while using their stick in one hand, Fallon and Maguire have a loose rein between the other hand and the bit. It suits them and they get results, but you must remember they both use great strength through the saddle via their legs and body to keep the horse running straight and stretching for the line. It is not a style which I would suggest to a novice rider for fear that the horse would drift off a straight line or simply try less.

No matter what your style is in a finish you want to keep the horse balanced, and that is very difficult to achieve if you bounce around from one side to the other and flail your legs like windmills. Your body movements need to keep within the horse's stride pattern and if you watch the best riders they do this neatly. When a horse gallops it is like a spring, stretched out and extended one moment, with one front leg – the lead leg – landing on the ground slightly ahead of the other. The next moment the horse coils up as its body and back legs catch up with the front legs. In effect the horse's body is going down and up as it goes through these two movements and if a rider gets excited in a finish they may lose synchronicity with the horse's stride. Instead of pushing their hands forward and lowering themselves in the saddle as the lead leg stretches forward, and then bringing their hands back and easing their body upwards as the horse coils up, they do the opposite with the result that you get a bouncy and unattractive piece of riding. Most horses can gallop with either their left or right leg leading – if a horse gallops around a right-handed bend it should lead with its right leg and vice versa. Some horses seem to want to lead only with one leg, and if that is their right, then they are almost certainly better galloping on a right-handed track.

Really pushing a horse for the winning-post comes after niggling, when you simply squeeze the horse and nudge its neck. At this point I often give the horse a slap or two down the neck while keeping my hand on the reins – this makes a cracking noise but does not hurt the horse and usually gains a response. If I need to see if there is more in reserve, I show the horse the whip by waving it by their side in rhythm with their stride pattern; as their lead leg and head extends forward, the whip goes forward too, as the lead leg folds underneath, the whip comes back to just behind my leg. Showing the horse the whip before hitting them behind the saddle is a requirement of the rules of racing now and often generates more impulsion from the horse. If that carries you to the lead then waving your stick is adequate, if it does not, then you have to give the horse a crack.

When doing so some jockeys prefer to keep the stick protruding from the bottom of the hand past the little finger in what is known as the 'back of the hand' position. Others prefer to 'pick it up' so that it protrudes forward between the thumb and forefinger, a position offering more versatility and more force. Either way it must be kept below shoulder height, reducing the risk of hitting too hard.

Bearing in mind that you must give the horse time to respond I like to wave the whip twice and if that fails to elicit a response I use it behind the saddle high up on the rump, then wave it twice more and use it again. 'Is the horse responding?' you have to ask yourself. If not then hitting it 22 times will make no difference, but if your horse is digging deeper or quickening, then you are justified in using the whip again if needed. The rules no longer stipulate how many times you can hit a horse but common sense tells you what is hitting unnecessarily.

The common mistake among novice riders is to use the whip when their horse has no chance of reaching the first four. It is pointless hitting a horse in that situation, and while riders have to secure the best possible placing in order to satisfy the demands of punters and the form book, pushing with your hands and perhaps waving the stick are adequate.

What you should never do, although it is something which is seen on racecourses too often and must be stamped out, is to hit a horse rapidly in what we call the machine-gun method. This rapid use of the whip is invariably applied in the dying strides of a race when two or more horses are going flat out for the line. It was a method which Lester Piggott famously used on Roberto when he narrowly beat Rheingold in the Derby of 1972, an era when such whip use was regarded as satisfactory. Jockeys who use that style today are fined and suspended, yet this has not eradicated its use. I can state here that even if the Cheltenham Gold Cup was up for grabs and I was neck and neck with another rival on the run-in I would not use the 'machine-gun'. Not only is it unfair on the horse and breaking the rules of the sport, I have seen it put a horse off, causing it to lose its stride or shy away instead of extending in a straight line and pushing its head forward. Some of the best finishes I have seen involved jockeys who put their sticks down and simply pushed for the line, maintaining that crucial rhythm which keeps the horse balanced and running straight.

Being alert in a race is so important, no matter what your knowledge of a horse; you are not just in a little bubble, doing your own thing. Horses are all around and if you are daydreaming or focused purely on your horse you are either going to be a danger to your rivals or you will miss out when someone makes a tactical move.

There are blind spots, however, and shouts of 'keep straight' or 'give me room' are commonplace in races as horses wander off a straight line. This is bound to happen occasionally when 'the field' – the runners in a race – turns to go around a bend. Early in a race it is generally just a case of bunching, as those horses on the outside come across to shorten their route. However, in the latter stages of a race, perhaps on the final bend before the finishing straight, it is a much more cut-throat business and you see horses being checked as they try to take the shortest route. Grabbing 'the inner' – the point closest to the rail – can be a tricky manoeuvre and inexperienced riders often get it wrong, trying to claim it from behind when it is not theirs, or trying to hold it when in front after another jockey has seized the initiative. The rider behind has to decide whether the gap between the horse in front and the rail is big enough to go through and whether the horse has enough speed to claim the gap for itself. If the answer is no in both cases the jockey has to sit and suffer until the bend straightens and there is room to challenge the leader. You want to avoid being checked at this point because, although a rival who blatantly obstructs you is likely to be disqualified, you may have to prove that was their intention and not merely an accident. In addition, once a horse has been checked it has to rally and that is not easy when it is tired.

Bollockings get handed out in those situations, normally from a senior rider to a novice and occasionally verbal fisticuffs occur between riders of the same status. I would not recommend Kieren Fallon's one-off method of retribution. Kieren pulled Stuart Webster out of the saddle after a race and received a six-month ban, but as he has become champion jockey twice since he has obviously learnt from the experience.

My own introduction to the roasting came from Jimmy Frost, whose parents run a yard in Devon and are real stalwarts of West Country courses. Being keen but green I tried to push my horse up Frosty's inner in a race and while he closed the manoeuvre off, he waited until we were back in the weighing-room before telling me I was a half-witted moron, or words to that effect in slightly stronger language. The weighing-room fell silent although I'm sure the other jockeys were sniggering like hell and I felt myself growing smaller by the minute. That was daunting and humiliating but it made me think very carefully about trying the same move again and no doubt was a good lesson.

I have said good race-riding begins at home and there are two other key areas which can be achieved away from the race-course: fitness and form book research. Anyone who has not ridden assumes sitting on a horse is like sitting in an armchair, it is far more strenuous than that, and race-riding is probably more demanding than any other equestrian discipline. Comparing a hack along the lanes with riding in races is like comparing a walk across the office to the coffee machine with a marathon.

Working with horses will engender a level of fitness, but getting to peak fitness is a matter of personal taste. As I mentioned in the chapter on diet, muscle is three times heavier than fat so the last thing I would want to do is lift weights. For me, getting fit means tightening up the muscles already in place and getting my lungs working and blood circulating. Running and cycling help do the job but there is nothing better than riding horses at home and in races. Some jockeys swear by mechanical horses, which, as the name implies, are horse-shaped machines on which you place a saddle and bridle and which enable a rider to strengthen leg and upper-body muscles. A mechanical horse can reproduce much that is similar in race-riding – and if there is room indoors, jockeys can push away on their metal steed while watching TV or listening to the radio.

The aspect of riding in races which I believe is critical, is the preparation you can do through study of the form book, which gives you an idea of what might happen when the tapes go up. No matter whether there are three runners or 30 runners, you must do your utmost to be aware of each horse's capabilities.

Imagine the scenario where a jockey is booked for a favourite in a five-runner race but fails to make time to do some research. Sitting quietly in behind, all is going well until the horse in front hits a fence, turns a somersault and brings the favourite down. Later the irate trainer berates the ill-prepared jockey for following a horse which had hit the deck in two previous races.

That is a very simple example of why homework is important, but there are many other more subtle reasons why studying both your horse's and the opposition's form is so vital and can save blushes after a race. By sifting the information you can find out which horses are likely to make the running, which ones are likely to appreciate the prevailing ground, which are likely to struggle for stamina, which have shown a good turn of foot at the end of their races. By knowing these facts you can discuss tactics with an owner and trainer before a race. It is a jockey's dilemma when, having been told to keep his horse at the back of a field, he finds everyone else is trying the same tactics and a very slow early pace is unfolding. If the jockeys have done their research and warned the trainer this could happen, they are in the clear if they abandon Plan A and make the running instead.

My own homework involves a thorough read of the form for every race I am riding in, usually on the night before a meeting, and then a quick skim through the form in the *Racing Post* when I arrive at the course. Also, this proves beneficial when I am offered two rides in a race – by having a general grasp of the form book I can quickly make a decision. The issue becomes less easy when riding an unraced horse, in which you are relying on the trainer to give you an insight into the horse's characteristics.

IX
The Big Meetings

The sport of jump-racing may be regarded as a winter event, but spring is emerging before the season reaches its zenith. There can be no denying that the season is now geared towards a few key events, particularly the National Hunt Festival at Cheltenham but also the three-day meetings in April at Aintree and Punchestown, and while there are some very rewarding pickings through the winter months, trainers would all like to keep something in reserve for the spring. Some say this concertinas the season, but I do not see it that way and believe racing benefits by putting on these key festivals which challenge other sports for a place in the public eye. Besides, trainers and owners are not so stupid as to completely shun decent prizes in the first half of the season, it is just that if there is a doubt about running a horse, perhaps because the ground is extremely heavy or just too firm, you cannot blame them for taking the view that keeping a horse in one piece for Cheltenham is the priority. Owners get such a thrill out of having a runner at the Festival, which is a wholly unique experience at a magnificent venue, it's natural that this should be their first choice.

The prize-money is very tempting too: as the year 2000 approaches, a minor race at Cheltenham is worth about £20,000 to the winner, many other contests at the same meeting are worth £30,000–£50,000 and the Gold Cup and Champion Hurdle are worth about £150,000 to the owner of the first horse before deductions. Any win at the Festival therefore pays a horse's training fees for a couple of years at least, and although there are only 19 races in which to pick up such a pay-out just about anyone who owns a jumping horse is hoping their animal is good enough to make the line up.

An owner or trainer who buys or breeds a horse which later becomes top class can make some serious money, particularly on the flat where a classic or group one winner can earn a seven-figure sum on the track and be worth several million pounds at stud. In jump-racing the rewards are not as great and even a really consistent horse like Desert Orchid, who won big races over a number of seasons, could only amass just over £400,000 in his career. That paid for his keep and made a decent profit but recent Derby winners have earned more than that for two and a half minutes' work. In addition very few jumping horses go to stud since most are gelded and the few who remain as 'entires' and earn fame over jumps will never make fortunes as stallions. They may produce quality jumping stock but not top-class fast horses who win big money on the flat, and that is reflected in the stud fees their owners can charge. Alderbrook, who won a group race on the flat – and was regarded as good enough to remain an entire horse – later won the 1995 Champion Hurdle and for the 1999 season he commands a fee of £1,500 each time he covers a mare. Lammtarra, who won the Derby, King George and Prix de l'Arc de Triomphe just a few months after Alderbrook's Cheltenham triumph, earned £30,000 each time he was put to a mare. He was later sold to Japan before his progeny could prove themselves on the racecourse, but the long-standing champion stud Sadler's Wells, a special case perhaps, has been earning more than three times Lammtarra's fee in recent years.

Stallion services can be a lucrative bonus for flat jockeys – if a jockey wins big races on a horse they have helped to boost its stud value and may receive a percentage of its yearly earnings from covering mares. Alternatively, or perhaps additionally, the jockey may own a few mares who can be covered by the stallion for no charge or at a discount.

I am not bemoaning the lot of jump-jockeys when making these comparisons, merely pointing out facts, but in our game money does not come along in really large lumps. Mind you, some decent winners at the big spring meetings at Cheltenham, Aintree and Punchestown, topped up with a win in the Irish and Scottish Nationals, would produce quite a financial windfall.

The jumping season, which begins with unseemly haste on

the first Monday in June, quickens up in November, a time which coincides with the close of the flat season on turf (all-weather racing continues through the winter months). Flat racing fans now have a major championship to look forward to at the beginning of November, the Breeders' Cup meeting held in North America, but once that has been held the attention of the media turns to the jumping game. All jockeys have to be grateful for the chances they get no matter how small, but by then we are all ready to ride some decent material. The job is simply more fun and offers better rewards when you are working at a higher level and while October meetings at Chepstow (which is usually televised), Kempton and Wincanton can attract the odd good horse, the two-day midweek meeting at Cheltenham at the end of that month is the first sign to me that the covers are coming off. If the autumn is wet and the ground good there will be some nice horses running by then, but it does make for a long season and some horses simply don't have the constitution to be at a peak over so many months. You cannot go to Cheltenham or Aintree with a tired horse, one who has gone stale by the months of routine work on the gallops. To counter that, trainers often talk of giving a horse a break to freshen them up, which could mean a week or two of taking life easy and perhaps spending an hour or so each day out in a paddock. Some horses love time in a field and whinny to be let out in the fiercest weather, while others seem far less happy and stand by the gate waiting to be taken back to their stable.

That late October meeting at Cheltenham is a wake-up call. If Britain's premier jumping track is ready for business, then we should all be too, and if the ground is right the top horses, and those who have the potential to be that good, will be ready for their seasonal debuts. In contrast the lesser-grade horses, often firm-ground specialists who have been racing through July, August and September, will be ready for a break. Some will have rattled up winning sequences and climbed in the handicap accordingly, and that weight burden, allied to softer ground and the emergence of better-class horses, will almost certainly halt their victorious march. They will be 'roughed off' (given a holiday), particularly if the skies appear full of rain, until re-emerging in the spring when the ground tends to dry out again.

Traditionally the first major showdown of the jumps season is the Murphy's Gold Cup which is run at Cheltenham in mid-November. Formerly the Mackeson Gold Cup, it is a contest which has captured the public's imagination simply by being the first real test of class chasers, although its kudos was not hindered by a catchy title. Everyone in jump-racing would refer to 'The Mackeson', which, after 36 years, had become ingrained into the pattern of the season. The brewery which sponsored the race decided on the name change and as 'The Murphy's' I doubt it has lost any ground – the title is still easy to remember and conveys an image of the battles between British and Irish horses which give jump-racing another dimension. Yet for all a sponsor's attempts to boost a race's image, the final decision about its place in folklore will rest with the horses which win it; in the case of the Murphy's the roll of honour includes: Gay Trip, Bachelor's Hall, Bright Highway, Half Free, Bradbury Star and Dublin Flyer, all top-notch performers who could really draw crowds to the races.

The Mackeson was once the highlight of a good day but I doubt anyone really remembered the other events on the card. Yet Cheltenham, through its managing director Edward Gillespie, often leads when it comes to marketing racing, and the Murphy's is now the centrepiece of a mini-festival which offers something for many tastes. It is a three-day meeting and the Friday card, known as countryside day, includes numerous site attractions and a cross-country chase. This event may not appeal to purists but it is a new concept and it certainly offers some decent money for a tranche of horses who are clever and agile jumpers but perhaps a gear or two slower than ideal. They now have an additional goal, which is good news for their owners, and the early runnings of the race have given the public the chance to see horses from the Czech Republic, where this type of race is more common. Whatever your views about such add-ons to the Murphy's meeting, it shows racing is looking at new ideas and being positive by trying to pull in both the racing community and the paying public.

The Becher Chase over Aintree's Grand National fences and a decent card at Ascot follow on, but the next really big meeting in Britain is the Hennessy fixture at Newbury. The Hennessy

Gold Cup is a long-standing sponsorship and a very important handicap chase run over three and a quarter miles, a distance which means potential Gold Cup horses join the line-up. Arkle, who dominated jump-racing in the mid-sixties and remains the best chaser in the sport's history, is among past winners of the Hennessy, and it is invariably a race to make the skin tingle.

Newbury is, for me, the best jumping track, it presents a very fair test for horse and rider. The fences are big but the races are run at a good gallop and there is plenty of room, because it is a wide track, so you get little bumping and boring. There are no hard-luck stories; the best horse wins and it takes a good one to capture the Hennessy. For that reason it is a real quest for a jump-jockey and I was chatting recently in the weighing-room with Richard Dunwoody when the subject of big races came up. Woody has won just about every feature event in the calendar and can have no regrets about a dazzling career, but he admitted he would love to add a Hennessy to his portfolio.

Riding at Newbury, and also at Haydock which is similar in design, requires patience because from the turn into the home straight there are still almost six furlongs to cover. At most other courses you need to be in contention on the final bend but when I rode Sharpical to win the Tote Gold Trophy, a major hurdle run at the track in February, we were last at that point. That was not altogether planned but Sharpical had plenty in reserve and that was the number one priority when the winning-post was so far away.

It is the lure of the home turn and the desire to be in a good position at that point which may account for the mistakes and falls which occur at the cross fence at the far end of the course. Jockeys who are near the front feel they must hold their prominent position as the others bunch up getting closer to the action, but I feel it is better to let a horse sort itself out there and concede a few lengths, rather than worry about a big leap and maintaining or snatching some ground. There is plenty of time left and there are four more fences to jump.

At around the time of the Hennessy, the better two-mile hurdlers, those who will be chasing the Champion Hurdle, get a chance to win a prestigious prep race: the Fighting Fifth Hurdle run at Newcastle. While a week later the best two-mile chasers, who have the Queen Mother Champion Chase on their agenda, are invariably sprinting around Sandown in the Tingle Creek Chase, a competitive contest named after a very classy chaser of the seventies. The Rehearsal Chase at Chepstow gives Gold Cup horses a chance of further action and then it is back to Cheltenham for the Bula Hurdle and a valuable chase known lately as the Tripleprint Gold Cup. Ascot's valuable Saturday card precedes Christmas and then all sights are focused on Boxing Day and one of the highlights of the season.

The King George VI Chase, which is run over three miles at Kempton, is a championship in its own right, a showdown among the best chasers at that distance whose owners are attracted by a race steeped in tradition and that offers a prize of nearly £70,000 to the winner. The winner of the King George VI and Queen Elizabeth Diamond Stakes, a major flat race run at Ascot in midsummer, picks up about five times that sum, and I am sure owners of jumpers would love to pursue that sort of cash, but the thrill of winning Kempton's big race is about more than money. It must be, otherwise people would not bother to own jumpers and would instead be racing solely on the flat. Winning a King George and having a horse which follows in the footsteps of such as Arkle, Wayward Lad and Desert Orchid, is to take a place in racing legend. As a jockey, an owner, a trainer or a stable lad or lass, that feeling of achievement will survive when the prize-money is long gone – and that £70,000 can pay the bills for several seasons and buy a new horse or two.

I am an unashamed fan of Christmas and look forward to it each year. There is a special feeling about that time of year which some hate and others love. I am firmly in the latter category. If a jockey has stayed free of injury and suspension they are ready for a break by that time and the festive period usually means three or four days off work while racing shuts down. Stable staff do not have the same perk and go on tending to their horses, but they do get some additional time off. If Christmas Day is on a Saturday even better, because that means having the Sunday off as well and being able to indulge in some turkey, stuffing or a mince pie. The jockeys' Christmas dance is one of the first events of that period, a really good evening which attracts riders from far and wide to a hotel near

Lambourn. Then, after a lazy day or two and a bit of shopping, Jane and I usually go down to her parents' home in Devon. The prospect of the racing in the week ahead is never far from my mind.

Unless the weather is particularly bad there is always a good crowd at Boxing Day meetings, whether at Kempton, Wincanton or Wetherby, and that adds to the challenge and pleasure of the day. The television cameras are rolling too, and that always gives a jockey a lift. Being on TV is like having your own advertisement, a chance to show how good you are, and if you ride a winner there is the bonus of being shown in the replays which follow. People ask whether we try to look neater and more stylish when a meeting is being televised by the BBC or Channel 4 but there is a bigger agenda than merely looking the part: winning is more important. While we all avidly watch the replays in the weighing-room after riding a winner, most of us cringe at our efforts and you hear groans followed by a rider saying, 'Oh, no. I looked like a sack of potatoes.' I have never worried about the cameras and most of my colleagues feel the same, but they seem to motivate Paul Carberry who simply has to try something out of the ordinary. Paul is a character and a brilliant jockey, known in the weighing-room as Alice after his favourite song, 'Living Next Door to Alice' by Smokey. This tune first became a hit in the seventies and has become an anthem in Ireland, played at parties, weddings and probably divorces and funerals too. It is hard not to smile when a couple of hundred Irish men and women, buoyed by drink, stand as one and roar the chorus, 'Alice! Alice! Who the f**k is Alice?'.

Winning a race at Kempton on Boxing Day is not quite Cheltenham, but it is not far from it in terms of achievement and, with a very good supporting card which includes a tip-top novices' chase, there is plenty at stake. The King George stands out, however, and it really is a spectacle and generally run at a very good pace. People say that because Kempton is flat then the race is suited to horses who only just stay three miles, but I don't hold with that view – it is run at too strong a pace to suit non-stayers. The class of the horses means that everything happens faster than in an ordinary race; the front-runners really bowl along and because it is a tight track they are always turning the bend which tends to make them race close together to save ground. This in turn makes them work just that little bit harder. If there are two front-runners on a straight track and racing apart from each other they are not pressuring each other to turn up the gas but at Kempton they can't avoid each other, so the pressure really mounts. The good two-and-a-half-mile chasers, who invariably run in the race, are cruising in the slipstream and the whole race is a thorough test from start to finish and you must have stamina to last up the home straight. While people say the King George has little relevance to what might happen in the Gold Cup in March, I am not so sure. True, the Gold Cup is run over a further two furlongs, on a left-handed undulating track with a stiff uphill finish. But the undulations do mean you can get a breather into your horse, particularly running downhill, which is not the case at Kempton. People have this image of Cheltenham being a real stamina test over a very stiff course and suiting stamina-laden horses, but nothing could be further from the truth – particularly at the Festival where big fields invariably mean you are tight for space and need a nimble horse who can jump quickly and has the speed to hold a position; exactly the type of horse which excels at Kempton. You rarely get big clumsy horses winning at the Festival but if they have a powerful engine they will have their day at Newbury and Haydock, where the long straights give them a chance to unleash full thrust. If a punter wants some advice from this jockey, it would be follow Kempton form at Cheltenham – I think it will pay off.

The feast of festive racing continues after Boxing Day when Kempton stages the Christmas Hurdle, but a bigger prize is on offer at Chepstow where the Welsh National over three and three-quarter miles is often a very dour battle among staying chasers. In spring and autumn when the ground is on the firm side, Chepstow is an easy track for horses because it has plenty of long downhill runs. Yet when it gets wet in winter it is one of the toughest courses in Britain and, with the Welsh National attracting classy competitors which increases the likelihood of a fast pace, the winner often needs to stay at least four miles to be successful. This seems to suit certain runners who become real Chepstow specialists, and a number of racetracks have this habit of appealing to horses who can win there but hardly anywhere else. Towcester, with its very stiff uphill finish, Ascot with its stiff fences and short home straight, Chepstow and Kempton, for reasons mentioned earlier, are all good examples of courses which produce track specialists.

Once Christmas is finished the Cheltenham Festival is just ten weeks away. Older, good horses will have been aimed at that meeting since the start of the season, but no one can be sure of their novices until they have performed a few times. By early January most young horses have shown their mettle and are either on the list for the Cotswolds or not. If a novice has been held up by the weather or an injury it may look like a Cheltenham horse but it won't be considered experienced enough for the big meeting and may have to wait another year. In the meantime there are good prizes on offer in prep races for the Festival or at events which stand up in their own right. The Mildmay, Cazalet Memorial Chase at Sandown in early January is one example, while the Ladbroke Handicap Hurdle at Leopardstown, run at the same time, is a very valuable handicap and major betting event which usually attracts runners from Britain. The Great Yorkshire Chase at Doncaster in late January offers a decent prize in the north.

Many Cheltenham hopefuls have a pre-Festival run in February in races like the Hennessy Cognac Gold Cup at Leopardstown, the Tote Gold Trophy at Newbury and the Racing Post Chase at Kempton. There are also a couple of valuable Grand National trials during that month, too, at Uttoxeter and Haydock.

Then March arrives and every minute of every day is countdown time, as trainers and stable staff nervously check their charges, jockeys privately hope they avoid an injury and owners ensure their tickets are sorted for the greatest three days of racing in the world. The Imperial Cup at Sandown, held on the Saturday before Cheltenham, is a traditional and valuable hors d'oeuvres for the main meal and then it's off to the feast we go.

Well, nearly. As the Festival is always held over three days beginning on a Tuesday – it is interesting to note that they moved the Derby to a Saturday to gain more coverage but the

Festival is an absolute sell-out as a midweek event – but that means there is a tricky Monday to get past beforehand. Typically, there are three meetings held that day, usually one or two on my stamping ground. Even though Nicky is loath for me to ride in case I take a last-minute knock I prefer to do so as I always feel a little bit stuffier on Mondays when I've had Sunday off and so a couple of rides just gets everything in tune for the three days that lie ahead. I am not nervous about the risks of having a fall which would rule me out of the Festival, but it is only natural that you consider the possibility and pick and choose what you ride accordingly. That fussiness, the decision to shun horses who are prone to careless jumping, applies for, perhaps, two weeks before Cheltenham, but there is no guarantee what will happen in a race. Wayfarers Way proved that at Wincanton on the Thursday before the big meeting in 1996. A sensible young horse who jumped well, I had ridden him in all his schooling sessions at home and felt confident in his ability. Taking part in a 16-runner maiden hurdle, I kept him near the back of the field before getting into contention three jumps from home and, moving smoothly into the lead at the second-last, I was ultra happy with the way things were going. I still don't know what went wrong but he ignored the next hurdle, went 'splat!' and gave me a mother-and-father of a fall, one which could be shown to young jockeys as the epitome of the dangers in the sport, and just what you don't want to be doing in the week before Cheltenham.

If a man can be called lucky for breaking his collar-bone so many times that he has to have it partly removed, I am that man. The right-hand bone had been weakened by breaks and because a third of it had been removed there was nothing to snap when I hit the turf, so, although badly shaken, I was able to resume riding the following day and made it to the Festival.

Cheltenham is quite simply the most important event in this job, a showcase for the talent of horses, jockeys, trainers, breeders, stable staff, sales companies and sponsors. If you have an association with jump-racing then you want to be a success at the Cheltenham Festival, and it is very depressing for me to have drawn blank in both the 1997 and 1998 runnings of the event. I walked away from those two meetings feeling absolutely green with envy and utterly miserable. That is how the Festival gets to you.

I suppose it hits me harder now than at any time in my career. I am regarded as one of the country's top jockeys and am therefore expected not only to perform on the big stage, but also to take the lead role and ride a winner or two. Not that I am alone in suffering the ghastly anxiety which creeps up on you as the Festival comes to a close and you still await your first winner. Peter Scudamore, seven times champion jockey, went for years without reaching the winner's enclosure. My own feelings of loss were amplified in 1997 when Nicky ran two horses in the last race of the meeting, the County Hurdle, and I elected to ride one purely out of loyalty because the owner was not happy about one or two issues and the boss and I agreed it was an appropriate way of keeping the peace. My gut feeling was that the other runner, Barna Boy, had the better chance and he duly galloped to victory under Richard Dunwoody. That hurt, that really did hurt, and I don't think I have ever felt so frustrated about fate's fickle ways than I did driving home that night.

Cheltenham is great for jockeys and spectators, although the jockeys are pretty much cocooned away from the razzmatazz going on among the 50,000 spectators who travel there each day. My mother and brother generally come over from Ireland for the duration, but I hardly get to speak to them because it is so busy. They simply have to join the crowd, one which bets, shops, drinks, eats, dances to various bands and struggles to move about the course. The meeting became so popular, particularly Gold Cup day on the Thursday, that a limit had to be placed on admission.

For most racegoers the horses are the centrepiece of the whole event, but I have heard of people who attend for three days and never see a horse in the flesh at all, preferring to stay in the bars and restaurants where they place bets and watch events on TV screens. This seems a pity because Cheltenham racecourse, or Prestbury Park to give it the official title, is an unforgettable location offering a wonderful test of both horses and jockeys and it is set amid one of the most aesthetic views that can be seen from any sport's venue. I cannot look across the course without being aware of a feeling of majesty, as though the champions who passed through left a legacy of their greatness. Fill the place with spectators, officials, bookies, horses, vehicles, stable staff, newsvendors, catering and bar staff, trade stands and the countless other groups which make up a day at the Festival, and you have created a memorable event. Rumours that Ireland empties for three days are not far wide of the mark.

The atmosphere in the weighing-room is pretty good too. It is one of the infrequent occasions when all the top riders from both Britain and Ireland congregate. Throw in a continental jockey or two, any amount of amateurs and conditionals, and it is a place that is bursting with expectation and excitement. Just about every race is a championship, so there is plenty at stake. There is tension too, and a cacophony that never recedes, and while you might think there would be a hush of expectancy before the three biggest events – Tuesday's Champion Hurdle, Wednesday's Queen Mother Champion Chase and Thursday's Gold Cup – it never gets a chance to descend. Half the lads that are to ride in these will have been taking part in the previous race and they stream into the weighing-room like waves rushing up the beach and for a few minutes the place babbles with discussions about the contest just ended while television replays are scrutinised. All the while there is a frantic scramble to rip off one set of colours and pull on the next lot, to grab a new number cloth and check weights before going through to the clerk of the scales for the official go ahead. Then there is just time for cap-tying and an open discussion on who is going to make the running and then it is back out to the paddock. At a normal midweek meeting you might be greeted there by just the travelling head lad, although the owner and trainer usually attend. But Cheltenham is special, an occasion not to be missed. Each owner seems to bring family and friends, and as the paddock is impressively large and with all the people cramming around its edges to get a glimpse of the runners, it is unlike any other pre-race gathering. Once in the saddle you become a jockey, there to do a job, but you cannot help but feel the throng, as though the weight of the crowd is squeezing the air and if your adrenaline is not motivated by that, you are myopic or made of ice.

Some horses sense the occasion too and become excited, but

most know what to expect yet, unless they have raced at the Festival before, they will not know of the enormous wave of sound which builds like a roar from the stands when a race begins in earnest at the top of the hill. With racegoers packed on either side of the track, the runners have to run up a funnel of people and the sound which cascades across the track must carry halfway back to Dublin. The Irish love horses and racing and they pack the place – when one of their own, particularly a well-backed runner, begins to get the upper hand in a race it is as though they are picking Cheltenham up and banging it on the ground. Is there any wonder jockeys get such a thrill from riding a winner at this great event?

To receive the accolades from your beaten colleagues is a great feeling and then to ride back to the winner's enclosure, knowing you have earned a place in history, would warm anyone's soul. The smiling stable lad or lass and travelling head lad are invariably the first to greet you as you ride back in triumph, then it is into that wonderful enclosure where the first four are unsaddled. The crowd claps and cheers with gusto, the cameras whirr, you touch your cap in acknowledgement and allow yourself a punch at the air and then it is down into the back-slaps of the owners, the interviews with press and TV, the accomplishment of another dream.

Reality dawns soon after and as 50,000 people are all trying to get out of the place at the same time and, assuming I don't have a ride in the last race, it is time to get packed up quick and hightail it out of there. Sitting in a traffic jam for hours is murder, particularly when you want to get home, have a bath and an early night. There is no time for celebrating now, there are horses to be exercised tomorrow and a race meeting to ride at in the afternoon. Besides, the season has not finished just because Cheltenham is over – the Grand National is only a couple of weeks away.

Aintree's three-day meeting is a terrific event now, with lots of very good supporting races and decent prize-money on offer. A number of Cheltenham runners take part, but the two events are quite different, each with its own atmosphere. Cheltenham is dominated by racing people while Aintree seems to attract a crowd which is less discerning, often quite young, but definitely there to enjoy a good day out. The Savile Row tweeds and quality brogues make way for Liverpool fashion – and if that is mini-skirts and platform shoes, or Armani suits and Ralph Lauren shirts, so be it. You certainly see some memorable sights.

I have no problem with modes of dress, but I was taken aback on one occasion at Aintree after suffering a fall from a horse called Tinryland. As he went down and I rolled across the turf, a hoof caught me below the belt and I was rendered gasping for breath and in some pain. While lying in the grass, my hands placed at the point of pain, medical help arrived and asked if I was okay. Wincing through screwed-up eyes I saw a woman's shoes and tights and the hem of a nurse's skirt. 'I've been kicked in the bollocks,' I gasped, and she responded by gently feeling for damage.

After a few moments she asked me to sit up, which I did, and she carried on rubbing my back while offering words of comfort. Maybe it was the tone of voice, maybe the face was rather square-jawed, but it suddenly occurred to me that all was not as it seemed with this nurse. She, I suspected, was a he, perhaps a cross-dressing member of St John Ambulance or a member of a stag party in the process of winning a bet. Either way I suddenly felt much better, clambered to my feet, shunned her offer of a lift in an ambulance which was on its way and headed back to the weighing-room as fast as I could.

As a jockey I want a full book of rides on each day but getting a mount in the National is naturally top of the list. Not having a ride in an event which is a national obsession, and having to watch it on television in the weighing-room, would be like a kick in the guts, although I am very lucky that as a past winner my name seems to be linked with good horses in the run-up to the race. If Nicky has a runner the chances are I will be on it, no matter whether it is an outsider or not, but failing that my agent Dave Roberts does his best to get me on a horse with a decent chance.

Aintree uses two sets of fences – the National fences are the large, spruce-covered variety unique to the track which are used for one race on each of the three days of the meeting, while the Mildmay fences are typical of the birch models seen at all other courses. They are used for the cognoscenti's highlight on day one: the Martell Cup Chase, which often attracts horses which contested the Gold Cup. That is followed by the Fox Hunters' Chase, a chance for amateur riders to tackle the National fences.

As I mentioned in an earlier chapter, some amateurs are excellent riders and among their ranks will always be good youngsters learning the art before turning professional. Yet I don't suppose they mind knowing that we crowd around the telly in the weighing-room when they go out to ride in this race, and unless a few of them are ballooned into the air or sail across a fence while their horse stays on the take-off side, we get very disappointed. Call us sadists if you like, but we are only human and most people would find a race like that entertaining – especially if there are some spectacular exits from the saddle. The fact that the amateurs get out there and have a go typifies what so many people love about jump-racing. And if anyone says the National fences are easy now, and that modifications have detracted from the skill requirement, I suggest they buy themselves a horse and have a go. True, some of the high-risk elements such as the ditch on the landing side of Becher's Brook have been removed, but the fences still have to be jumped and the distance of the Grand National, four and a half miles, will always be a challenge. It only took heavy rain and very soft ground to reduce the number of finishers in the 1998 race to six, which suggests it is still a tough challenge. I believe it is a fair one too.

The Irish Grand National at Fairyhouse in mid-April and the two-day Ayr meeting, featuring the Scottish Grand National, five days later are the next big targets for jump-racing stables. I felt disappointed when they reduced the Scottish fixture to two days, because Ayr is a fair track – like Chepstow a real test of stamina when wet but an easy course when the ground is dry – and by that time of year there is precious little racing left for good-class horses, particularly if the ground begins to get firm. If a horse has been on the sidelines because of injury, then the Ayr card might be their last chance of a run and a three-day meeting offers a greater range of races.

The Whitbread Gold Cup, Britain's oldest sponsored race dating back to the 1950s, offers top-class chasers one last big prize, and, as a handicap but of similar value to the King George

VI Chase, it often attracts Gold Cup and Grand National horses. Yet the Whitbread comes at the end of a long season and that, allied to the weight which good horses have to concede, means that it often throws up some long-priced winners and some very disappointing efforts from short-priced favourites.

Three days later the roadshow crosses to Punchestown in Ireland for an event the organisers are happy to call the Irish Cheltenham. A three-day meeting, it has been boosted by some serious sponsorship money and great improvements to the facilities which help attract good horses and a very large crowd. Trainers and owners based in Britain are treated royally by their Irish hosts and for many it is a fitting way to complete the season – a case of serious racing and serious socialising.

By May most class jumpers are enjoying a holiday. Flat racing is dominating the scene again, with the first of the season's Classics, the 1,000 and 2,000 Guineas, taking place at Newmarket. For the jumping fraternity there is racing most days but it is lower grade and any fireworks tend to be concentrated in the championships for the leading jockey and trainer. If two or more jockeys are in a close finish for the title it adds interest to the closing weeks and if the protagonists turn up at Stratford and then go to Market Rasen's evening meeting on the final day at the end of May, the impact of the season is held until the end.

X
The Rules

If you have passed a driving test you are supposed to know the Highway Code. If you are a jockey you are supposed to know the Rules of Racing, a neat little tome, almost 400 pages long and a riveting read best kept in the smallest room in the house. The Highway Code is funnier.

The Jockey Club, which has little to do with jockeys and everything to do with racing's rules and regulations, is the author of this publication and also the arbiter in disputes. If we need advice in deciphering a rule we talk to the Jockeys Association or an official at the races, but it is not much use asking for help or reaching under the saddle for a copy of the book when you have a wall of horses around you and a big prize is at stake. Instead, we make ourselves aware of the crucial issues and attend seminars when a major change requires a question-and-answer session. We may not need to know about pony races, Norwegian graded stakes, the neurectomy operation or masters of hounds certificates (which all merit a section in the book) but we do need to know when we can get back on a horse which has fallen, about restrictions on bypassing jumps and whether a horse declared to run in blinkers has to wear them. Getting it wrong can lead to disqualification, which is a bitter taste, and a hole in the bank account.

Of all the 'Orders and Instructions' which govern racing, that known as H9 is one of the most emotive. Instruction H9 refers to use of the whip, and no matter whether you ban it or ban the restrictions on its use you will never please everyone. It is constantly being written about in the press and seems to haunt all riders at some time in their careers.

I could not agree with banning the whip, a useful aid which

does no damage if used correctly and sparingly, and I believe the guidelines which tell a jockey what they can and cannot do with it are clear and accurate; anyone who breaks them deserves to be fined and suspended. Yet it has sickened me on occasions to see the abuse given to some horses in races, fairly rarely, thank God. The Jockey Club is not happy with such incidents either and is taking a strong line on over-zealous whip use.

I write as a man who has been banned for misuse of the whip and knows what is at stake. In the 1991–92 season I broke the rules twice in a week, but I was a good bit younger then and relatively inexperienced (I was still claiming a 5lb allowance for being a novice rider). I realised I had to adapt and keep my cool and, while I'm as tough as the next man and tougher than many, I now only use the whip when I'm getting a response – if a horse gets tired and is metaphorically 'going backwards' then you can hit them a hundred times and it won't make any difference, although it might sour them for good.

Some might say it is easy for me to be critical when I am in the fortunate position of riding for respected trainers on good horses owned by people with enough money to be in the sport for pleasure. Some jockeys find themselves riding for trainers who are under pressure from owners who, in turn, are under pressure from their wives who think the money could be spent on something else. It is not easy trying to get a moderate horse to win or be placed and when a jockey and trainer are under pressure it is often then that the whip gets overused.

Grey areas abound on this subject and one of the most nebulous surrounds the marking of horses. The difference between the hair and skin on horses is as varied as the hair on human heads – some people have thick, glossy hair, others have wispy, thinning hair, and there is no doubt which offers more cover. In horses the term 'thin-skinned' means just that, and while two animals may look identical from a distance, if you grip a piece of their skin between your thumb and forefinger you could find a great disparity in robustness and depth. It also explains why some horses stand stock still while being groomed and others twitch frantically, contort their flanks and often kick out in their efforts to get away from the ticklish brush.

Similarly, a jockey can give one horse a couple of cracks on its rump which won't turn a hair, while on a thin-skinned horse the same action would result in lumps appearing under the hair. Such lumps attract the attention of the racecourse vet and if they feel the markings are the result of unnecessary force then the jockey and trainer can be summoned to the stewards' room where a penalty may be handed down. In a bid to prevent such cases and to help jockeys, a list of horses known to be thin-skinned is circulated. If a horse is not on the list but proves to mark easily because of its skin texture the trainer can be fined.

Once I know a horse marks easily I use a special air-cushioned whip; several designs are now on the market, the first having been designed by octogenarian farmer and owner Jim Mahon. They are not always as effective or well balanced as conventional whips but, in addition to sparing thin-skinned horses, they show the stewards that you made an effort to be sympathetic even if a mark does appear.

The Jockey Club is doing its best to solve contention involving the whip. It is not fair that a horse should win a race while their jockey breaks the whip rules, yet neither is it fair to disqualify a horse in those circumstances because that would penalise the hapless owner, trainer and stable staff. Punters, too, would feel aggrieved if a horse they backed was disqualified because of an over-zealous jockey, yet they are not happy now when a horse they back finishes second to a horse whose jockey has broken the rules.

Possible penalties which have been discussed and might work include: disqualification of horses or the denial of a jockey's percentage if they are found guilty of whip misuse. The latter idea has some merit, but with the sums involved in racing these days, both in prize-money and stud fees for horses which win big races, jockeys who lose their percentage may well be paid later by grateful connections. Unethical, true, but when there is a lot at stake people find ways of circumventing the system.

The people who monitor the use of the whip and all other rules on the racecourse are known as stewards. If they feel a minor infringement has taken place they may simply have a quiet word with a jockey or trainer; if something more serious occurs they instigate an inquiry and use video evidence. They have the power to fine and suspend people and may refer a matter on to a higher authority at Portman Square in London, the home of the Jockey Club, if they feel their own powers inadequate. A sequence of infringements, known as the 'totting-up procedure', may mean that the stewards on a racecourse are duty-bound to send a person to Portman Square.

I feel sympathy for the stewards who often face very difficult decisions, but consistency is sadly lacking on occasions and there are courses where you know the stewards make the right decisions and there are courses where you know the stewards are prone to making gaffes. At present, stewards are drawn from the local area and offer their services for expenses. Critics say professional stewards are needed, and doubtless they will come in time, but at present the best officials are those who rode in races – not just a few amateur or military affairs, but regularly on a professional basis. They understand how unpredictable racing can be and have a better feel for the job.

What is annoying is when an incident develops which has no precedent and yet the stewards hand out a penalty drawing upon a rule to justify their decision and banning a blameless jockey. That happened to me at Taunton several years ago and I am convinced it cost me a Hennessy Gold Cup win on Rough Quest; he finished second, but I still think my knowledge of how best to ride him would have made the difference. I definitely missed a win on Conquering Leader in the valuable stayers' hurdle run just before the Hennessy and all because I was suspended for seven days by the stewards at the Somerset track after they decided that I was guilty of taking the wrong course – along with five other riders.

A new and worthy rule had just been introduced allowing fences and hurdles to be bypassed if a horse or rider is lying on the landing side, usually because they have been injured on the previous circuit. Prior to the introduction of this rule jockeys were supposed to steer their horses over the jump and avoid doctors, vets and ambulance staff who would be working away on the far side. It was an accident waiting to happen.

At Taunton I was partnering a horse called Rainbow Walk for John O'Shea and was some way behind the leaders when it became apparent we would have to bypass the last hurdle. I had been given an idea this might happen having seen a horse fall at the hurdle on the first circuit, and I remember noticing how he had sprawled left as he went down. Approaching the hurdle I saw the leaders bypassing it on the right, and while I knew we were supposed to do so on the left, I assumed that route was blocked by medical staff because of the way in which the horse had fallen.

You can imagine my shock, bearing in mind this was a new rule and you would expect a little tolerance, when I, Tony McCoy, Mark Richards, Guy Lewis, Tom Dascombe and Emily Jones were hauled before the stewards and given a week's holiday while the first four home, who all went to the right of the hurdle, were disqualified. I accept our mistake was enhanced by the fact that four jockeys did go to the left of the hurdle and therefore were promoted to the first four places, but being disqualified seemed harsh enough in the circumstances and the six of us decided to appeal against our bans by taking our case to Jockey Club HQ in London. We were turned down.

Two other rules which keep them busy, and of which we as jockeys have to be particularly aware, concern non-triers and interference, which can found in the book under rules 151 and 153 respectively. If you can imagine the hurly-burly of a race, the many responses of the horse to being in a bunch of galloping rivals, varieties of ground, weather, racecourse, distance of race and preparation, it is hardly surprising that 151, the 'non-triers rule' as it is known, should be observed so closely. Its *raison d'être* is to ensure that punters get a fair deal from racing, the theory being that if punters lose confidence in betting on horses they will desert the sport and take their valuable cash elsewhere. Rule 151 is designed to ensure every horse is trying to win – without it there would be nothing to stop trainers using the racecourse as a schooling ground or giving their horse an easy race either to reduce their handicap rating or to improve their odds for a day when the money is put down with the bookmakers.

It has to be said that horses have run in races in those circumstances, but the Jockey Club is cracking down heavily on anyone who does not run their horse 'on its merits' and the rule clearly states that jockeys have to 'take all reasonable measures' to win or obtain the best placing. With almost every race in Britain now being shown live on cable or terrestrial television and improved camera shots available to stewards at every meeting, the Jockey Club has put in place a system which makes it very hard to bend the rule.

There are times when a horse does not perform to its best ability, often for a totally inexplicable reason, and it is then that the stewards' secretary will have a quiet word. If the jockey has a good answer, perhaps that the horse hated the ground or needs blinkers, and their words are borne out by facts, the information may be relayed to the public. If, however, the explanation is not satisfactory, an inquiry will be held. The trainer, or a representative, has to attend these inquiries and while they may not be able to shed light on the horse's performance, a test to see whether the horse has been doped will almost certainly be carried out. The stewards may also hold an inquiry if a horse wins a race after finishing well behind in its previous run. Again, there may be genuine excuses and the jockey simply has to remain above board with the answers.

It is the grey areas which make the rules unpopular, and the non-triers rule is open to some subjective interpretation. Take, for instance, the situation where a jockey is nursing a desperately tired horse, punch-drunk as we call it, towards the line knowing that third place is the best they can hope for. With the post a few strides away the jockey eases off and the horse slows dramatically, quicker than the rider would have expected, at the same time, another horse, galloping on the other side of the course and out of earshot of his rival, comes with a late burst and just snatches third spot. The jockey who was sympathetic to his mount and eager to stop pushing as soon as possible, suddenly finds himself guilty of infringing rule 151, even though it would be harsh to say he did not try to gain the best possible placing – he did – it was just that a combination of events made it look otherwise. From being a sympathetic person who is looking after a horse, the jockey is suddenly a rule breaker facing a suspension which could mean missing a big-race winner.

In most cases like that the jockey has to accept the blame, but sometimes horses make life very difficult. I was involved in such an incident at Wincanton recently, and while the stewards exonerated me of blame, the *Racing Post* headline the following day read 'Fitzgerald is under fire'. The article said I 'incurred the wrath of punters', although that was a little far-fetched. Riding a free-running mare called Coh Sho No, I built up a long lead over my three rivals, hoping to burn them off and last until home. The favourite, Solvang, under Richard Dunwoody, closed me down turning for home and jumped ahead at the last hurdle. He pulled away so easily at that point that there was not a person on the racecourse who would bet against him, and I stopped pushing my horse knowing she had given her best and we were well clear of the third horse. But as soon as Woody stopped pushing Solvang he slowed dramatically, allowing my mare to close him right down. In fact I almost ended up his backside. Some people said that if I had kept pushing I might have snatched the race back, but that would not have happened because Solvang had plenty of petrol left and would definitely have rallied – Woody would have made sure of that – if my mare had got alongside. That said, I accepted that the incident did not look good to the public, many of whom are genuine racing fans but who never ride horses and could not fully appreciate the subtle ways in which they operate.

Non-triers covers a multitude of sins, from blatantly stopping a horse, to failing to race a horse with sufficient effort, to the schooling and conditioning of a horse (giving it 'an easy') in a race. In the first example the owner/trainer and jockey risk being 'warned off', banned from all racecourses for many years; in the second a trainer is fined, the jockey suspended and the horse suspended from racing for 40 days; but the last issue is less clear. What is certain is that it would have some trainers from the past turning in their graves. Giving a horse 'an easy' has been part of racing for centuries, and while it can be connected with betting it is also part of educating young horses or bringing injured horses back to the course. A temperamental youngster who has a tendency to get wound up and have a brainstorm, could easily be brought to this state of alarm if put in the front line on its first run. In the front line the pace is hot, there is a fair bit of jostling for position and the sound of whips cracking and hurdles rattling can be quite frightening. In an easy introduction, the young horse is started near the back, given an opportunity to jump in its own time and pick up confidence through running past a few tired rivals in the finishing straight. While that sort of experience would not completely pacify an equine wild-child it would mean that you could up the ante in its second and third runs and expect the horse eventually to learn to channel its energies into the business of racing. With horses coming back from injury, a similar reasoning applies, the idea being to get the racing muscles operational and to blow the cobwebs away while gradually putting pressure on the injury – too much pressure, too soon, could result in the damage flaring up again.

Another reason a trainer might want to prevent a horse running to its best ability is connected with handicapping and betting. Once a horse has progressed through novice races it moves into handicaps and, in theory, gets more weight to carry each time it gives an improved performance. Eventually this weight rises to a point where the horse finds it hard to win. It simply cannot concede weight to other horses who are on their way up the handicap. It may have to run several times, or maybe more, before its rating is reduced by the handicapper. If a trainer and their owners want to win a decent prize and have a bet on that horse at some point in the future, they stand a far better chance of completing their aim if the horse has sunk in the handicap – preferably to a point some way below its real mark. Some of the many ways of doing that, of artificially getting a horse down the handicap, is to run it when not fully fit, on unsuitable ground, over an unsuitable distance or without blinkers. With a bit of help from a co-operative jockey who looks as though they are trying hard but are not really getting to work, a horse's handicap weight can be reduced. Some of these ways are breaking the rules, some are bending them, others might be classed mere gamesmanship, but some trainers and jockeys struggle to make a living and if an owner is putting pressure on them they may feel forced to get involved.

The rules have always said horses must try to win, but the difference for trainers and jockeys today is clear – they used to get away with giving a horse a gentle run but it is much harder if not impossible now. They must give every horse in every race a chance of winning and if that means a jockey has to refuse a ride because a trainer wants it to have an easy run, then, in theory, so be it. Jockeys will find themselves in some difficult situations.

Giving a horse a conditioning run to help it gain peak fitness, something I was asked to do several times when I began riding, is no longer allowed. Jockeys have to be active in the saddle and trainers can no longer use races as part of a training programme. There was a time when they could openly say of a horse before a race, 'He is not fit and will be better for the run.' Or, if a horse had a quiet run after a lengthy enforced rest and then won its next race, they could say, 'He needed the run badly last time and was fitter today.' In both cases it could be said their horse was not racing to win – or is it saying a horse is trying to win but it is not fit enough to do so? It is yet another grey area and one which the rule book can never clearly define, particularly when horse welfare is of prime importance.

It is a fact that a race makes horses exert themselves more than any amount of training at home, but that is probably true of humans too, the person who trains on their own and runs for miles on the streets will always run faster and push themselves harder in a stadium in front of thousands of spectators. Horses do win on their first run in a race or after a long lay-off because they are superior or better prepared than their rivals, but they cannot be driven to maximum fitness purely by working them on the gallops at home. Yet racing badly wants to hang on to punters and to prevent them becoming disillusioned and drifting off to bet on other sports. Every horse must now be trying 100 per cent – at one recent jockeys' seminar this was forcefully put to us. The Jockey Club is clamping down and we all have to be aware of that fact but I believe they are doing the right thing. Racing must be seen to be scrupulously clean – not only for the benefit of people who back horses regularly but also so that we attract newcomers, those people who live under the misapprehension that racecourses resemble Graham Greene's book *Brighton Rock*, where gangsters wait to nobble horses and that fixed results are part of the war with bookmakers. Stories of illegal betting coups may add to the colourful history of racing, but in an increasingly sensitive world where sponsors and television companies like a clean, wholesome product, it is a benefit to all in the sport if we clear out malpractice.

One answer may be to experiment with a scheme called 'schooling bumpers' which works successfully in Ireland. These are 'races' in which there is no betting and horses can therefore be given as much work as a trainer and jockey deem necessary. They are held on normal racing days so the horse gets a taste of the job. In Britain trainers are merely allowed to give their horses racecourse gallops which involve two or three horses from the same stable working together, a very different scenario.

Interference caused when horses get in each other's way in races (rule 153) tends to happen more on the flat where distances are shorter and a greater number of contests finish with horses bunched together. It is in the burst for the finishingpost that a jockey, trapped behind their rivals, pushes their horse through narrow gaps, sometimes legally, sometimes not. On other occasions a horse simply wanders or diverts dramatically from a straight line and that too can cause interference. In jump-racing the same scenario happens, often when a horse gets tired, so strength in the saddle can be a real virtue then.

When a case of interference takes place in a race the stewards have to ask themselves how bad or wilful the jockey's actions have been. Using a sliding scale they consider first whether the jockey is guilty of reckless riding; if not then they consider intentional interference; if not they look at irresponsible riding and finally careless riding. If the jockey is innocent of all these the interference is almost certainly accidental and there will be no penalty against the jockey if it is proved that they tried to prevent the interference or matters took place beyond their control. However, and this is crucial to a jockey if a win is at stake, the placings will be altered if the interference affected the placings. In other words, if a horse shies from the whip and brushes another horse but wins by ten lengths it has almost certainly not affected the placings – on the other hand, if it only wins by a head, beating a horse it brushed which had to be pulled back before rallying, then it will almost certainly lose the race.

I have been lucky in avoiding too many inquiries into such issues, although I had to endure one when I won the Grand

National on Rough Quest and it was not a nice experience. In that instance the stewards decided that although my horse had drifted in front of a rival any interference was accidental and had not affected the result.

My own experiences of stewards and the other officials found on a racecourse are that they are normal people trying to do a job. I have not always felt their decisions were correct but I cannot remember feeling they were ever petty, biased or vindictive. They see us on a regular basis so it is best for all concerned to keep relations friendly. I have been told off by a starter for saying too much on a couple of occasions, as have most jockeys, but it gets pretty heated when the horses are about to come into line and such incidents are quickly forgotten.

If a jockey feels hard done by and wants to appeal against a fine or suspension the Jockeys Association is usually contacted and the issue run through with the secretary Michael Caulfield. His experience generally gives him a good idea as to whether an appeal will succeed and since an appeal costs £300 and there is the time and money spent in going to Portman Square, it pays to take his advice.

Over and above the normal rules involved with riding in races there are also restrictions on jockeys which are designed to keep racing clean. We are not allowed to bet, the theory being that we might be tempted to fix races if we stood to win a lot of money from bookmakers, and in a bid to tighten up racecourse security and prevent horses being tampered with the rules forbid us sharing information with people who are termed 'undesirables'. Over and above the penalties which the Jockey Club can hand out, such as fines and suspensions, the police may be called in and criminal proceedings started if a jockey breaks a law of the land.

In 1998 the police interviewed and held on bail three jockeys, Leighton Aspell, Jamie Osborne and Dean Gallagher, while investigating allegations of race fixing. In January 1999 three more senior racing figures were arrested – jockeys Graham Bradley and Ray Cochrane and trainer Charlie Brooks. The police inquiries were continuing as this book was being published, although Aspell and Osborne had been cleared of all charges. Nonetheless, at the time of their arrests we could not help wondering who would be next. In fact, the more absurd the accusations, the more it made jockeys feel vulnerable to the finger of suspicion.

The issue made all jockeys aware of the need to keep their eyes open and walk on the straight and narrow – it is not a crime to talk to people but you had to wonder whether you were being watched. The case involving Jamie seemed ridiculous. It centred on a race at Exeter when he rode a horse called Avanti Express which later proved to have been doped. I was at Exeter that day too, and remember it was a pretty wet and miserable occasion when you needed a bit of luck to get round and would have been a lunatic to start sticking substances up your horse's nose. After his arrest, and those of the other two jockeys, we all just prayed we didn't ride a doped, beaten odds-on favourite in a race involving irregular betting patterns, which was what happened to Leighton after he had ridden a horse called Lively Knight at Plumpton. He then had to endure the embarrassment of being hauled in for questioning and was hit with a legal bill in order to defend himself. The final outcome to this case had many permutations, but what it did prove to me was that the Jockey Club's Security Department is active and, in an industry in which millions of pounds change hands every year, it is best to keep yourself to yourself and remain above reproach. Better to earn an honest penny than a quick but illegal quid.

Fortunately, I have never been asked blatantly to stop a horse by someone I knew – although I did receive an anonymous phone call at my home soon after I became stable jockey at Seven Barrows. I was about to leave for Leicester races when the phone rang and a man asked me to stop a fancied horse I was due to ride. 'There will be good money in it for you,' he added. My reply was an emphatic 'no', although the culprit got his way because the horse was beaten on merit. I have no idea who the call came from and because it was at a busy time I did not report the incident. But because of increased vigilance and greater publicity about such matters I would inform the authorities if anyone ever tried again, as would my colleagues, of whom I know one or two who have been offered similar bribes, all flatly refused.

XI

The Future

Jockeys are affected by or are at the centre of virtually every bureaucratic change in racing and there have been some important ones in the time I have been riding.

As this book is being prepared for publication a major development, the seemingly never-ending saga of jockeys' sponsorship, should reach a conclusion. It has been deliberated over for ten years and been a real slog for the Jockeys Association and secretary Michael Caulfield. His negotiations have involved the Jockey Club, British Horseracing Board, the Racecourse Association and the Owners Association among many and covered a vast range of issues and arguments.

As I have already mentioned, a jump-jockey's career can be short and even the top riders earn nothing like the salaries to be gained in other high-profile sports, so maximising earning potential is not about driving sleek cars or living in mansions, it is about doing enough to make a living and hopefully putting some money on one side for a life out of the saddle. Increased television coverage, including cable, satellite and digital transmission, means that jockeys are being exposed to a very large audience and sponsorship is a logical way of supplementing our income. A company name carried on the breeches seems to be the way in which this deal will finally be witnessed by the public.

Depending on who you talk to it seems to be the consensus that jockeys have not been used to promote the sport in the past and it is time for change. Frankie Dettori is being used in a campaign to market the Tote and racing is definitely waking up to our potential for talking to the public about the sport we love. Whether sponsors will expect us to take a leaf from boxing and be depicted as gladiators, to emerge from the weighing-room in whirls of smoke and spotlights and to walk to the paddock over a bridge above the crowd while a deafening blast of 'We are the Champions' or 'The Final Countdown' reverberates around the racecourse, I doubt. It really isn't racing's style.

Yet our potential to create interest in this sport and to attract people to watch it and spend money on it is gradually being realised. Ask any kid about football or cricket or rugby or boxing and they will talk about Michael Owen, Shane Warne, Lawrence Dallaglio or Prince Naseem, even though all those sportsmen take orders from coaches, trainers, managers, financial dealers and sponsors. In racing too, the people who market the sport are realising that we can do a job of promotion. We want to be paid, of course, but that is the commercial world we now live in. There has been a reluctance in racing to accept this and while the horse will always be the centre of the public's affection, and greats like Arkle, Nijinsky, Red Rum, Brigadier Gerard, Desert Orchid and Cigar deserve to be on a special pedestal, jockeys are the side of racing with which everyone can empathise. They see our triumphs and failures in the same way they view those twin aspects in other sports.

The JAGB believes jockeys can be used in a wholly beneficial way for the sport and I remember Michael Caulfield's wry smile when John Sanderson, clerk of the course at Doncaster, said it was imperative that the top jockeys should be available to ride in the St Leger at his course. His comments came after a host of top jockeys missed the Classic in 1998 – Frankie Dettori, Pat Eddery, Mick Kinane and Olivier Peslier rode in the Irish Champion Stakes, while Kieren Fallon was in action at Goodwood. Sanderson was pleased for John Reid, who substituted for Dettori and won the St Leger, but he knew the public wanted to see all the top riders. Who knows, maybe one day jockeys will receive appearance money and while I don't expect it to happen during my career in the saddle, who could say for certain it won't – and that would be pure anathema to many!

All changes have their pros and cons and the recent additions to the calendar of summer jumping and Sunday racing have also caused plenty of debate. In their present format I am unhappy with both. Summer jumping, racing during June and July, means we now race 12 months of the year and it is too much. Until 1994 there was no jump-racing in those two months, but there are now meetings on about three days a week in that period which gives us no chance for a proper break. It is not as though this is a job which allows you to coast for a month or two – if you do not aim to be 100 per cent fit and mentally prepared for every ride you are a risk to yourself and your horse and you could cost punters money, which, whether a selling hurdle at Bangor or the Derby, is something the authorities will not tolerate.

As a traditionalist I miss the passing of a close season for jump-racing, primarily because it was an ideal time for jockeys to patch up niggling injuries and to allow the body a complete rest from the daily routine. It also meant getting a lie-in for a few weeks and, as one of the heavier riders, having a break from the mental and physical torture of dieting. While jockeys have to be enthusiasts, and I am very much of that mind because I love the job, a good break put zest back into the routine and there was a real feeling of optimism as the new season approached, an attitude which seemed to say, 'Great, I've had my holiday, visited the relatives in Ireland, got my golf handicap down, caught up with the accountant, the dentist and all the odd jobs that needed doing, I'm feeling fit – now let's get back to the horses.'

Since racing in June and July is not held on a daily basis there are chances to catch up on pressing issues, but as most people will confirm, a day off in the week is not the same as a two-week holiday, and for anyone in a demanding job the latter is a necessity.

Others who benefited when racing closed down included the horses – who were guaranteed some time in a field – the valets who look after the jockeys, and a whole host of other people who work in the industry, notably stable staff. Those people still get a holiday but it now has to be taken at a time that fits in with other staff rather than at a clearly defined time. For trainers there was a chance to wind their stables down for a few weeks and to catch up on outstanding business before they too grabbed a holiday.

A look at the stables which patronise summer jumping quickly indicates that few of the big yards are actively pursuing the meagre prize-money on offer, but there is no doubt that many new trainers see it as a chance to get established and since they will be in business when today's premier trainers have retired, a trend is being set.

If racegoers turn up and pay to watch this form of jumping, and there is no doubt fair-sized crowds do form on sunny days, it is hard to say we should scrap it, but I and many other jockeys are not advocates of it in its present guise. Many of us ride at these meetings not through choice but through obligations to trainers who support us in winter. Not that my availability is simply about altruism to owners and trainers. It is a competitive business, one in which other jockeys are hungry to take any rides which I might forego, and while I am loyally treated by most yards it would be a fool who took this for granted. So I smile and remain committed while wishing we could return to the old system in which racing shut down on or around 1 June and stayed that way until 1 August. Flat jockeys have faced a similar issue in deciding whether to race through the winter at the all-weather tracks, and while many of the top riders don't bother and others only do so very sparingly there are differences. They have no need to chase the scraps of the all-weather winter season because prize-money in their summer job is good and they have the bonus during that busy period of winning big prizes on the continent on Sundays. They can also ride abroad in the winter, in places like Asia and the Far and Middle East, and so combine a bit of sunshine and some work; and they can easily ride into their late-forties or early-fifties which gives them many more seasons in which to earn fees.

Quite apart from anything else, when a close season prevailed there was a great atmosphere at the season's final jumps meeting, held at Stratford, and having said cheerio to the valets and various colleagues we were all able to put our feet up – after attending a few end-of-season parties.

The whole business revolves around the dilemma of how much money a sport can raise and at what cost to the competitors. It is an issue in all sports and while the dangers of overkill are constantly debated, the bureaucrats never seem to make any thought-provoking concessions. I simply don't remember hearing an event organiser say, 'No, we won't stage this fixture, the athletes come first.' If there is a chance to make money from the public that is their priority and who cares about the long-term consequences for the men and women at the centre of the action.

Many of the top riders agree with me that summer jumping in its present format is a nuisance. True, we have a choice about whether we ride, but only so much as anyone else who says, 'No, I'm not going to work today' – a quick route to the dole office. And since this is a sport which requires very high levels of fitness, both to improve the chance of winning but also to lessen the chance of injury, and since many of us fight an ongoing battle with the scales, if we are asked to ride one horse at a meeting it makes sense to look for others.

As I mentioned earlier, summer jumping does open doors for some, helping new trainers and providing cash for hard-up jockeys whose winter earnings are not enough to tide them over through the former close season. I have no wish to deny those people a living but I do wonder whether we stretch our resources too thinly, and, while in the wet summer of 1998 there were plenty of runners and some competitive races, the general standard of the horses competing is poor. In a dry summer, when the ground becomes rough and quite firm, some races are contested by a handful of very mediocre horses and offer little appeal to racegoers or punters.

Putting on mini-festivals would be a better option, and while the courses at Market Rasen in Lincolnshire and Perth in Scotland are attempting to create meetings with a special theme they have yet to make a real impact. In order to do so they will need to bump up the prize-money for a couple of races at each fixture to attract good horses, create an image that these are championship races and hope that over the years they become embedded as events not to be missed. If they could link the big race at each of, say, three mini-festivals, so that any horse that scooped the lot would gain a bonus, the press would pick up on the idea and give it a boost. I know the press has only a finite amount of space and there is a lot of high-class flat racing at that time of year, but that does not mean jump-racing cannot raise its profile.

This summer festival idea has worked well in Ireland where the meetings at Kerry and Listowel and a bigger one held at Galway over six days are popular with the public and competitors. The Galway Plate, a steeplechase, and Galway Hurdle are very important races, rich in kudos and with very decent money for the first four. If Britain could put on a meeting to match this it would swell racing's finances through bigger betting turnover and be a far better format than the one at present which merely offers random meetings of little significance. And while it is likely the big trainers and top jockeys would farm the major races at these festivals, some events could be framed for trainers new to the sport or with small numbers of horses, and also for jockeys who had ridden a limited number of winners in the previous 12 months. The fillip they would gain from winning at a festival would be far greater than the current spin-off associated with capturing a joke race at Worcester or Newton Abbot. From a jockey's point of view it would be better to have a clear week with no racing followed by one with a festival. Centralising the racing at one location over several days means not having to do so much driving.

One benefit of summer is the chance of fine weather, and if the courses which stage a festival can offer camping and caravan facilities, plus accommodation in hotels and guest houses near by, and then put on events in the morning and evening such as steam rallies, country fairs, concerts, midnight steeplechases, parties or barbecues, they could become events that are not to be missed. If the public could get a reduction for attending all three festivals you might develop a wandering band of racegoers from a section of the community who have never been racing before. Many people with lots of leisure time or with flexible working hours could be attracted to racing.

I doubt these events would damage attendance at the big flat meetings such as Royal Ascot, Glorious Goodwood and York – they are established and rather grand occasions where people dress to be seen and the racing is for connoisseurs. The summer jumping festivals would be less formal but with the racehorse as their central theme.

One other unforeseen aspect of summer jumping is the effect it has on the ground at those courses which stage racing all year round. To get reasonable ground in summer the courses have to water them and this is bound to upset the equilibrium if we then get a wet winter. False, boggy patches are just one result of this attempt to put on racing 12 months of the year and it could be that courses will have to choose whether they race summer or winter, but not both.

Sunday racing I dislike even more than summer jumping, although I and many of my colleagues again feel the format is wrong, not the concept. A lack of prize-money and low-class racing seems to be the hub of the problem. What is the point of jockeys, valets, stable staff and lorry drivers working on their day off and trainers being forced to pay staff extra wages just to put on six forgettable races contested by moderate and poor racehorses? Surely everyone involved in racing, whether professionally or as a spectator, needs more of an incentive than to be offered such moderate fare, particularly when it follows a decent day's racing 24 hours earlier on the Saturday.

Good crowds do attend Sunday meetings if the weather is pleasant, and if some newcomers become owners as a result of the experience that would be no bad thing. Evening race meetings, which can be attended by people heading out of the office, have been a good way of enticing newcomers. What Sunday racing is clearly not offering when it provides such moderate contests is an attraction for betting-shop punters, so it is not generating worthwhile funds for the levy, the money taken from bookmakers to help fund racing, a sum of around £54 million in 1998.

Sunday racing was popular on the continent long before it became legal in Britain, but there they put up big money and stage feature races, keeping owners, trainers, jockeys, staff, punters and racegoers happy. While I appreciate we have a pattern of races which cannot be wrecked by introducing new ones just for Sundays, some sort of compromise needs to be reached.

The issue of a day off in the week following a Sunday meeting also needs to be resolved. Imagine any other industry in which the boss walked into an office and said, 'Right, you will all have to work on Sunday but there will be no day off in lieu or extra pay.' Stable staff quite rightly get a bonus for working Sundays but jockeys and trainers do not and there is still no firm agreement about letting racing close down for a day in the week following a Sunday meeting. The logical day would be Monday, but the obsession with keeping betting shops open and providing fodder for them seems to override all other considerations, even though statistics show that the most popular races to bet on are the better class ones with decent prize-money. I am not aware of a Monday race ever being among the most popular betting events of the year, with the exception of the rearranged 1997 Grand National won by Lord Gyllene when all bets placed on the Saturday were allowed to stand.

As ever, racing's many factions, from bookmakers to racecourses, race planners, marketing chiefs, owners, punters and jockeys, seem unable to agree on a plan to suit everybody, a legacy of dealing with an industry which is centuries old and riddled with ideals cast in stone. If we were to rip the lot up and give a clean sheet to some clear-thinking, rational and successful people from another industry it would be interesting to see how much of racing as we currently know it would survive.

That takes me to the question of the future, my own and that of racing, a sport and industry which seems to be getting better and better at promoting itself and winning battles for public affection. I know there are problems and that the recession hit all industries, but I believe the general position is good and with a business which dates back many centuries it is only natural there are some peculiarly dated aspects. Racing's strengths are its unique qualities: unusual but pleasing locations, colour and excitement of the sort which appeals to people of all ages and from all backgrounds, sport for the whole family, variety, international competition, gambling on something which can produce a very quick return, the spectacle of horses racing.

Man has put the horse to so many uses over thousands of years, from a humble beast of burden to a tool of war or transport for empire builders. In Western civilisations those uses are pretty much extinct now, although the horse is more popular than ever before on the field of sport. Partly for that reason, but also because of a change in the public's attitude towards animals, the welfare of horses will become an increasingly influential aspect of racing. The Jockey Club has already said it wants to make equine welfare a more important factor for stewards and that could lead to curbs on horses above a certain age being allowed to race, stricter regulation of horses before and after races and greater regard to the future of racehorses after they retire from the track. Retirement homes for thoroughbreds, run privately in the past, could receive far greater prominence and funding. Owners do not wilfully neglect their retired horses but at present no check is made on what happens to those horses if they are given away to a 'good home' and a few isolated cases of poorly treated ex-racehorses is bad publicity.

Commercialism will become a bigger factor as racing seeks to maintain pace with other sports and I expect we will see a stronger advertising presence on the racecourse and in television coverage. The sport already enjoys a very large slice of newspaper space in the mainstream press – whether that will always be the case is debatable and an increase in race meetings is already making some editors question whether they print all the cards. If they cut back it could be a cue for the launch of a daily sports paper which will pick up and develop further racing coverage.

Other aspects of the sport are hard to predict – this is a very old industry and change happens slowly. I would have said some of our smaller courses are in danger of closure but they all seem to have employed marketing people in recent years and are now using their resources to attract business outside of racing – as venues for functions, markets, car boot sales, concerts etc. Their futures seem more assured now, although the decision by Windsor and Lingfield to ditch jump-racing and concentrate on the flat, following Nottingham a few years ago, is a shame. Their loss might be another's gain if other courses are built in locations where racing is not so readily available. Sites in West Wales, Manchester and north of London are being investigated and each has merit if good people are employed who really understand turf management and how to provide decent ground.

The emergence of floodlit flat racing at Wolverhampton is an interesting development. Its Saturday-night fixtures seem to attract a new crowd, one which puts a priority on dressing smartly and enjoying an evening out with a meal and something to drink. If that is a market which is waiting to be tapped further then it should be, but it won't happen for jump-racing with the spotlights currently being used – they would create too many shadows at the jumps – but technology may well get round that problem one day.

Can anyone accurately predict the weather – one moment we seem to be heading for an ice age, the next we know drought is on the way? If we were sure of future rainfall it might dictate what type of horse we breed. The smaller, flat-bred horse became popular and successful as a jumps horse in recent years, but a wet period in early 1998 changed the advantage back to the old-fashioned, big-boned types who seem better able to cope with a gallop in the mud and they had a much better season. I hope we have several more wet winters because there are some very nice, big horses at Seven Barrows and their potential will only be realised if we get wet ground.

I cannot imagine many radical changes will happen during the rest of my career in the saddle, although I suspect there will be more racing at leisure times and more opportunities to bet – successive British governments have kept a clamp on when and where the public can bet, yet in many other countries you can walk into a bar or café and have a wager. That sort of facility will surely come to Britain in time.

In common with many sports people my career will be short and while I am still only 28, and pondering retirement purely for the benefit of this book, the mid-thirties is generally an age at which jump-jockeys decide they have jumped enough. The body begins creaking and offers less cushioning in a fall and once retirement is around the corner it inevitably becomes an issue; journalists want to be the first with the story once a sportsman or woman decides to quit and it seems to become a fascination for them – before you know it you are beginning to think about it yourself. The press seem to pursue the top flat jockeys more than their jump counterparts when it comes to this issue, presumably because flat jockeys carry on far longer and often ride into their fifties, and Willie Carson's impending retirement seemed to fill space every time his name was mentioned. Now Carson has quit the saddle it appears to be George Duffield's turn and when he won the 1998 Champion Stakes on Alborada the issue of retirement had to be a feature. George said he was happy and had no plans to pack in riding but I read one journalist who said it would be a great note to end on and this was typical of many.

Many people would like to know what future employment will hold and this seems to be particularly so of jump-jockeys. The job is precarious so it is only natural to begin looking ahead once you reach a certain age.

A top rider who retires after putting some money by should have a decent house and car and enough savings to set themselves up in a commercial venture if they wish – to date they do not quit with millions in the bank. Riders who do not figure among the top six to ten prize-money winners are unlikely to have the luxury of looking at business options, and while they may have a reasonable house and car they will definitely be looking for work when they retire. There are many options in the racing industry and I hope I will be able to offer my services. An involvement with sport of some description seems to be a prerequisite of any consideration.

Several ex-jockeys have successfully moved into coverage of racing on television and radio and that certainly appeals. I enjoy PR work and have always felt comfortable talking about racing in front of audiences and believe it is something I am reasonably good at – they say the Irish have the gift of the gab so I might as well put it to good use. There has been a trend in the media to co-opt sportsmen and women when they stop competing, but it may be short-lived and I could find there are no vacancies by the time I am ready to hang up my saddle. For that reason I am not agitated about what might happen and will simply look for any experience I can gain on the way. If my agents at RBI Promotions, who handle my business away from the track, keep me supplied with bookings to make after-dinner speeches and give talks at corporate functions then I will be practising and getting paid which seems a good deal.

I do not rule out getting involved in the bureaucracy and

administration of racing. Ex-jump-jockeys Richard Linley, Ron Barry and Peter Hobbs are employed as course inspectors by the Jockey Club, their job being to assess and advise on courses in order to maintain an even standard at venues across the country; while Robert Earnshaw, Phil Tuck and Paul Barton also work for Portman Square, their jobs being secretaries to the stewards who officiate at race meetings. Simon McNeill recently took up a position as starter. There are many other roles within the Jockey Club, and since it is an organisation with which I have had a good working relationship it may offer an option.

If I was planning to be a trainer, which is the choice of many of my colleagues, I would probably start thinking about a plan in the next year or two, preparing to court owners who could patronise my proposed yard and casting an eye on the property market.

I deeply admire a lot of trainers but I have to admit their job does not appeal to me at the moment, even though it is one way of maintaining daily contact with horses, still the best part of my job as a jockey. Training is a tough job and while I am not afraid of hard work the drain on a person's financial resources can be very damaging – someone with plenty of cash or a very committed backer should see a return on their investment but that is not guaranteed and it is getting tougher than ever to succeed without those advantages. Expenses such as wages, property maintenance and transport have never been higher, and you need top-class gallops, veterinary care and feed to compete with the best. Two or three years of high interest rates and a few bad debts can leave a trainer in the mire.

I know of former jockeys who are solvent as trainers, some operating profitably on a small scale by being very astute, buying and selling horses wisely, perhaps having a successful bet now and again and, most importantly, by gaining the support of loyal and honest owners. Having a very rich person as a patron may be okay for a while but if they don't pay their bills, or work in a business which is likely to crash, or choose to move their horses to other yards on a regular basis then they may not be much benefit to a trainer in the long run.

I have seen many ex-jockeys get into financial difficulties because they chose to become trainers. A good start on a small scale can quickly turn sour if the better horses are suddenly badly handicapped, a few get injuries and are retired, the soft-ground horses are held back by dry weather and firm ground, promises from potential owners are not carried out and the young horses bought at the sales do not find new owners and the trainer ends up owning part or all of them. Trainers must tear their hair out on occasions and while a big jumping yard with say 60 to 100 horses will have plenty of problems the amount of ammo they have means there is always something ready to go racing. All yards suffer lean times but one with just ten to 20 horses can be a very lonely place when times are hard and while that inevitably leads to a reduction in income from prize-money, it may also mean one or two owners remove their horses to trainers who are in fashion, having winners and gaining glowing press reviews.

When I started in this job I did not have a penny to my name so having saved a bit I count myself lucky. I have a great wife and a nice standard of living and would hate to lose that because a training yard became a drain.

The other factor which puts me off training is that having been associated with some very high-class horses at one of the country's top yards I would inevitably have to start some way down the scale, probably at the bottom. If a person has been lucky enough to race Ferraris it would be a hardship to sell, work on and maintain small family saloons, let alone be positive about their qualities to the public. Training is a seven-days-a-week job and if there were plenty of high-class horses about the place that would be a pleasure, but would it be much fun if the prosaic talents of a few handicappers were all that was available? I suspect it could become a real slog.

Not that the top yards have it easy and I never fail to be amazed at the workload which Nicky endures at Seven Barrows. He has some fine horses and terrific owners, but he is constantly busy sorting out problems, making phone calls and executing a thousand-and-one decisions. With that sort of pressure it is hardly a surprise when trainers beam with pride after saddling a big-race winner, and that is one benefit of all the hard work. It is difficult to think of many other occupations which can be so demoralising, yet so gratifying and rewarding – to bring a horse through a career to capture a Gold Cup or Champion Hurdle must be a fantastic experience. It is a real champagne or ditch-water existence.

That said, it would be a mug who turned down a very special offer out of hand and if someone put together a really exciting package which involved training I would have to consider it – but I am not holding my breath in anticipation.

Bloodstock agencies, feed and equipment suppliers, public relations and corporate work, transport – there are many avenues to consider linked with racing. I also have an ambition to buy a small-holding, a detached house with a paddock or two and some stables, somewhere for Jane to run a livery yard from home. It would be even better if we could buy three or four brood-mares and do a bit of breeding – I know breeding can be a way of losing money but this would not, initially, be a serious commercial venture, just a pleasant way of keeping involved. After all, it must be very satisfying to see a horse win a race and to reflect you chose the sire, helped foal the mare, weaned and prepared the youngster for sale. To take that plan a stage further, to keep the youngster and race it as an owner/breeder must be a terrific feeling each time it sets foot on the course. Who knows, I might one day breed, own, train and ride our horse in a race – that would be a rare moment for a professional jump-jockey.

Where this idyllic life will take place I cannot say for sure, but I suspect it will be Britain. Jane's family are based in the West Country and, while Ireland is my native home and I am proud of being Irish, I had nothing when I came to Britain and it has been good to me. Letting my memories wander back to those early days, I distinctly remember thinking that if I made it in Britain I would like to retire to the sun and that suddenly feels a good idea again. To have a place in Spain or Portugal, to take breakfast on the veranda before wandering out on to the golf course could be heaven. Perhaps I'll talk to Jane about the idea, while keeping quiet about the plans for golf. Whatever my future career moves I cannot imagine life without seeing a horse each day and if my next job means putting a collar and tie on it would be bliss to pull on the jodhpurs and riding boots and get in the saddle now and again – a good way of keeping fit too.

Working with horses is so rewarding, and to be involved with champions is a sublime feeling – so I hope there will be something for me in this great industry when I pass the winning-post for the final time. I have not regretted one minute of my time as a jockey, I am happy with every decision I have made and would say to anyone who wants to take up the profession, kick on and have a go.

Hopefully, I have a good few years left and some big winners still to come so, in the meantime, I will continue to live each day for the thrill of riding horses in races. I am just very happy not being a 'normal person'.

The Racing Channel

With over 900 race meetings featured annually, The Racing Channel offers the most comprehensive coverage of Flat, National Hunt and Point-to-Point racing ever broadcast.

The Racing Channel brings you live and exclusive coverage of up to three race meetings a day, from 11 a.m. to 6 p.m., Monday to Sunday.

Listen to the professionals marking your cards, make notes as you tour the top trainers' yards in our exclusive *Trainer Files* and enjoy the special features which provide a rare insight into the exciting world of horseracing.

Racing Channel subscribers also have access to a unique text service and benefit from a privilege card which offers hundreds of discounts on race-day entry, as well as many other special offers.

We provide a wide range of packages to suit your needs – including weekend or Saturday viewing only. For an immediate switch-on ring either:

0990-215-215 for Sky Analogue subscribers

0990-515-515 for Sky Digital subscribers

The Racing Channel is also available on cable. Please contact your local cable company for further details.